Sunset

ideas for great
kids' rooms

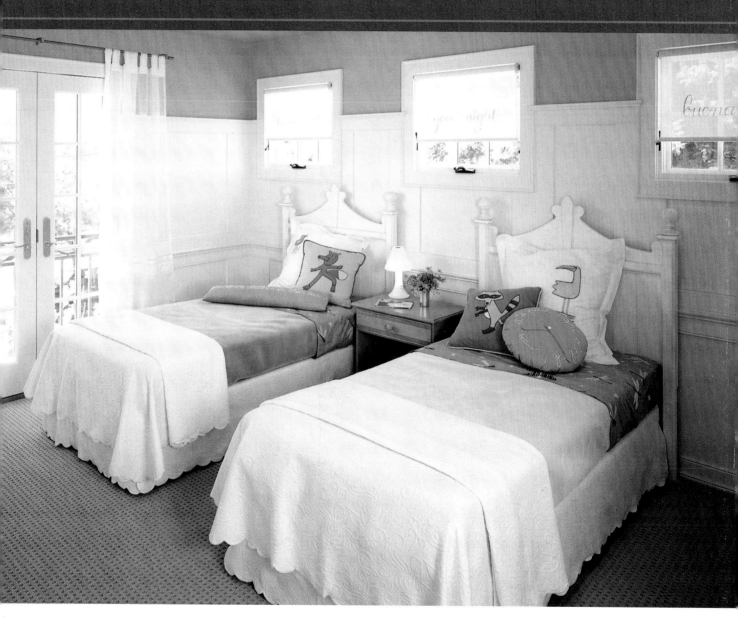

By Jane Horn and
the Editors of Sunset Books

Menlo Park, California

IfG
DESIGN

Sunset Books

VICE PRESIDENT, GENERAL MANAGER: Richard A. Smeby
VICE PRESIDENT, EDITORIAL DIRECTOR: Bob Doyle
PRODUCTION DIRECTOR: Lory Day
DIRECTOR OF OPERATIONS: Rosann Sutherland
MARKETING MANAGER: Linda Barker
ART DIRECTOR: Vasken Guiragossian
SPECIAL SALES: Brad Moses

Staff for This Book

DEVELOPMENTAL EDITOR: Linda J. Selden
COPY EDITOR/INDEXER: Phyllis Elving
PHOTO DIRECTOR/STYLIST: JoAnn Masaoka Van Atta
ART DIRECTOR: Susanne Weihl
ILLUSTRATOR: Tracy La Rue Hohn
PRINCIPAL PHOTOGRAPHER: Jamie Hadley
PAGE PRODUCTION: Linda M. Bouchard
PREPRESS COORDINATOR: Eligio Hernandez
PROOFREADER: Mary Roybal

10 9 8 7 6 5 4 3 2
First printing June 2005

ISBN 0-376-01761-9
Library of Congress Control
Number: 2003111884
Printed in the United States of America.

For additional copies of *Ideas for Great Kids' Rooms* or
any other Sunset book, call 1-800-526-5111 or visit us
at www.sunset.com.

Cover main image: Sally Weston, architect;
photography by Brian Vanden Brink.
Top left: photography by Thomas J. Story.
Top middle: photography by Eric Roth.
Top right: photography by Jamie Hadley.
Cover design by Vasken Guiragossian.

CONTENTS

HOW TO DO IT 89

Kids' Rooms Rule

No longer do kids have to leave home to get away from it all. Now they just go to their rooms. Once ignored by the design world or—worse yet—outfitted by adults who'd forgotten what it's like to be a kid, children's rooms are finally getting the attention they deserve. This newly revised title in Sunset's "Ideas for Great…" series opens the door to terrific rooms for kids of all ages. By the time you reach the last page, you'll have the information and inspiration you need to plan a room that measures up in every way—for you and for your child.

Many professionals, businesses, and homeowners assisted us by providing advice and information, or by opening their doors to our photo crew. We would especially like to thank Thomas Cutts of Ethan Allen, Emeryville, California; Lorraine E. Maxwell, associate professor of design and environmental analysis, College of Human Ecology, Cornell University, Ithaca, New York; Mary Cordaro of H3Environmental, Corporation, Sherman Oaks, California; Jamie Graff of Tapioca Tiger, St. Helena, California; Gretchen Gibson and Jillann Wood of A Child's Eye View, Oakland, California; Alla Kazovsky, architect, Los Angeles; Katie Quartey of IKEA, Emeryville, California; Cathy Smith of Goodnight Room, Berkeley, California; Danielle Kurtz of The Land of Nod, Wheeling, Illinois; Vasilios Kiniris of Zinc Details, Berkeley and San Francisco, California; Joanne Lim of Lighting Studio, Berkeley, California; Alta Tingle of The Gardener, Berkeley, California; Jonathan Straley of Jonathan Straley Design, San Francisco, California.

For the names of designers whose work is featured in this book, or for product sources, turn to pages 126–127.

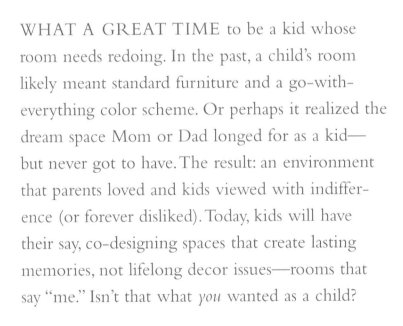

Rooms That Are
KID-FRIENDLY

WHAT A GREAT TIME to be a kid whose room needs redoing. In the past, a child's room likely meant standard furniture and a go-with-everything color scheme. Or perhaps it realized the dream space Mom or Dad longed for as a kid—but never got to have. The result: an environment that parents loved and kids viewed with indifference (or forever disliked). Today, kids will have their say, co-designing spaces that create lasting memories, not lifelong decor issues—rooms that say "me." Isn't that what *you* wanted as a child?

Whatever your budget, this book will help you design kids' rooms that not only look great, feel good to be in, and function beautifully, but also are rich in personal identity and character. Take notes as you tour "Ideas and Inspiration," a photo gallery and shopper's guide. Then use the "How to Do It" section to translate ideas and dreams into a workable, personal floor plan. Your child is eager for a new room, so let's get started.

Ideas and INSPIRATION

SUPER KIDS' SPACES—and the furnishings that
fill them—come to life in the following pages. You'll
find dozens of strategies for achieving the same goal:
creating a room for your child that's both practical
and a dream come true. This is a terrific time to fix
up a kid's room. Resources abound, from traditional
furniture stores to catalogs to Web sites. This photo-
rich section provides the ideas and information you
need to make thoughtful, stylish choices.

A Room
with a Viewpoint

MORE THAN JUST PLACES TO SLEEP, the best kids' rooms are so satisfying that the only thing their occupants really need to be happy in them is their own company. It's no surprise, though, that they want to show off such rooms. In fact, visitors of all ages are usually encouraged. What likely draws oohs and aahs from them is the final polish that comes from a unifying theme.

That doesn't mean that everything matches, which can be oh-so-boring. Instead, though it may not be noticeable at first glance, these rooms get their freshness from the way they blend function with a unique point of view. A kid's love of color might be wedded to a parent's passion for vintage furniture, or perhaps new uses might be found for everyday objects. Or the magic might result from carefully edited details like a gallery of self-portraits, or billowy draperies trimmed with sparkly beads.

The examples on the following pages offer a range of solutions, simple to sumptuous. You don't need a sky's-the-limit budget and endless square footage to give a room personality. Since children find satisfaction in the details, you can achieve this goal more easily than you might imagine. The message here is that there are many ways to make a big

Left: This room's preteen resident likes glitter, and Mom obliged with twinkly lights over the window, crystal trim on the curtains, and beaded wire camouflaging the lamp cord.

Right: To grow with the kids who live in this room, the playful birch plywood furniture is modular and interchangeable. Cantilevered pieces attach with slots, making them easy to rearrange—the footboard table also fits on the headboard. As a surprise for the two sisters who share the room, their mom installed a gallery of their self-portraits (bottom photo). Artwork hangs from bars with sliding clips—actually a kitchen storage system.

splash. Swathe the room in imported fabrics, or dress the bed straight from a catalog. Add character with antiques, or create accessories using equal parts imagination and glue.

The best kids' rooms blend function with a unique point of view.

Establish a sound foundation that can grow with your child. Start with a few well-chosen pieces of furniture that will support a child's changing tastes. Then add the "good stuff" from a kid's point of view—like a cushy comforter and throw pillows in favorite colors, a huge display board and plenty of pushpins, flop-down seating in the form of a squishy beanbag, rocket-ship curtains to frame a window, a dreamy canopy right out of a fairy tale. While the rooms you'll see in the next pages may not look anything like your kid's room, you can find inspiration in all of them.

Facing page: An upholstered chair and ottoman, flea-market treasures, offer more than just a cozy spot for reading. They're also props for play—they've served as everything from a queen's throne to a chariot. Their bright yellow fabric, repeated on the windows, will look great no matter how often the rest of the room changes.

Right: A hanging shelf keeps special things from being lost in clutter.

Above: A fun light fixture encrusted with glittery "gems" is a crowning touch above the room's closet.

A vibrant color scheme of hot pink, raspberry, and yellow looks sophisticated, not overly sweet.

Right: Think pink. The cotton-candy wall color avoids girly sweetness when paired with more sophisticated hues. A raspberry and lemon-yellow plaid on pillow and dust ruffle provides visual punch.

Below: A maple corner bookcase from the 1950s is paired with a mid-century vanity, complete with its original lights, for a stylishly retro look that won't soon be outgrown.

Above: A pair of white tieback curtains and cloud-patterned wallpaper put a "window" where there wasn't one before. The message board was created with green chalkboard paint.

Left: It's no surprise that this room has required few changes in eight years. Only the cheery blue quilt is new—everything else is vintage, down to the colorful rag rug.

Above: A cloudy forecast couldn't be more to the liking of this room's resident. Faux clouds were airbrushed onto a bright blue sky in three or four layers. Applying successive layers in opposite directions created wispy, diaphanous shapes that seem to move.

Left: Pegs display what's currently important or useful to the girl who lives here—from ballet shoes to purses.

13

Right: With furniture designed and created by their father, the kids who live in this house have rooms that are both private galleries and personal retreats. This minimalist canopy bed exudes maximum charm, its graceful arched support crowned with a petite scalloped platform that forgoes the usual swaths of fabric. The bed's whimsical carved, painted, and gilded touches are signatures of the custom furniture made by the father. A quartet of inquisitive faces surveys the room from the panel set into the footboard (below).

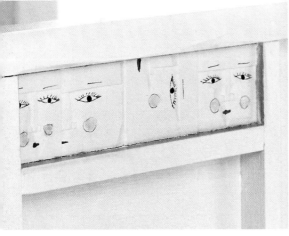

Right: Destined to be an heirloom, this sleeping retreat was handcrafted by Dad after his two-year-old son saw his sister's canopy bed (facing page) and demanded one of his own. With stars to dream on and pegs for hanging hats or golf bags, it still holds wonder for the boy—now a preteen. The huge white high-tops once hung over the entrance to a shoe store.

Facing page: The bed in this teenager's room, presented to her when she was four years old, is draped with sheer scrim panels nailed to a wooden frame hidden by a metal crown. Inside the canopy, a shiny mercury ball reflects its surroundings. The teen painted the walls herself.

Facing page: This room is a voyage of discovery for two brothers. Setting the stage is a huge map of the world, found in a catalog in an airplane seat pocket and ordered as a fun way to learn geography. A paperhanger installed it. The shipshape beds share a "gangplank" that is actually a runner set over wall-to-wall carpeting.

Above: At the foot of each bed, a hatch pulls open with the tug of a rope handle. Inside is storage for buried treasure such as favorite stuffed toys.

Right: Nowhere is reading more uplifting than in this cozy corner. Designed to resemble the basket of a hot-air balloon, it easily accommodates both boys and their dad for a nightly bedtime story. The step opens up to provide storage space.

For Display
and Play

PUPPET THEATER

Especially for preteen and older kids, it's their life story up on their walls—or at least the current chapter. Their interests and the latest trends change quickly, and what's cool today likely is cold tomorrow. The result? Walls dotted with pinholes, gummy with adhesive, or marred with the shadows of posters past. Encourage self-expression and discourage wall damage with a display board—as big as will fit.

Other display systems involve pegs, clips, and slots that serve as galleries for a changing array of artwork, practice schedules, and memorabilia. Use shelves to show off precious possessions like heirloom dolls or antique trains. While you're helping kids organize their collectibles, don't forget to organize some fun. Whimsical accessories give a room personality, and an imaginative touch like a tent or a puppet theater can create a little magic.

Board with it all

Corkboards are readily available in many sizes, with or without frames. A frame shop or online sources can fabricate one for you, if necessary, in a custom size. Or make one yourself; cork is sold as panels or in rolls that you can cut to size, and also as adhesive-backed squares or strips. Use cork to line doors, cover the side of an armoire, or fill the wall space above a desk. Designers often run cork up the full height of a wall in kids' rooms. Even pushpins are part of the decor now, with heads of clear or vibrantly colored plastic or decorative metal.

Magnet boards are proliferating—in many sizes, shapes, and even colors. Magnets allow instant rearranging, and there are no pins to pierce little fingers. There's even tape that is magnetized on one side, eliminating the need for visible magnets. With magnetic paint (see page 61), you can make any surface magnet friendly. Magnetic dry-erase boards accept both magnets and dry-erase markers.

A chalkboard can be a simple self-contained rectangle, part of an easel, or a whimsical shape. Hang one from the wall—or, with chalkboard paint (page 61), let it *be* the wall, or the facade of a door. If you have a pre-schooler, try to find a place for a chalkboard.

INDOOR TENT WITH TUNNEL

SHADOW BOX DISPLAY

Collage boards make charming, old-fashioned displays. Typically, these boards are wrapped with a pretty fabric and crisscrossed with ribbons to hold photos and other mementos. Look for collage boards in catalogs or at gift shops, or use a fabric from your child's room to make one.

Shelves, clips, and more

Attached to the wall at picture-molding height, shelves can show off treasures that might be damaged if displayed lower, closer to the day-to-day action. They are ideal for a doll collection, stuffed animals, or figurines. Run a shelf completely around the room, along one wall, above a window, or over a door.

For displaying artwork, organizers in the form of horizontal bars with clips let even little hands mount a one-kid show. You can make a similar setup by stringing clothesline across the wall and attaching clothespins. Shadow boxes hold tiny treasures.

Just for fun

What kid wants a plain-vanilla room? Punch it up and make it fun with whimsical accessories. Stir up an alphabet soup of letters on the wall. Hang a mirror framed with a bicycle tire to get the day rolling. Light up a window with a cluster of sparkly beaded flowers. Banish boring drawer pulls. Pitch a teepee. Start the show.

HANGING CHALKBOARD

4pm Soccer

WALL EASEL

FRAMED CORKBOARD

Bedtime *Stories*

KIDS OF ALL AGES love special beds that are also snug retreats. An enclosure of some form is the starting point for such dreamy sleeping quarters. Let it showcase the full bed or highlight just the spot where your child nestles her head. With fabric, hardware, and cabinetry—and, above all, imagination—you can create a bed that your kid will love to climb into and will remember forever.

What child doesn't dream of a regal canopy bed? You have many options if your princess wants to sleep like royalty. Hang a simple gauzy crown high above the pillow, or play dress-up with lavish amounts of fabric suspended from a dramatic upholstered cornice. Make a tentlike cocoon with colorful, super-cozy panels that open and close like hospital bed curtains. Catalogs and stores that specialize in children's furnishings also offer daybeds and four-posters already fitted for canopies.

A standard adult-size bed consists of a frame, a mattress, and a box spring. But for many small fry, climbing nightly into such a bed requires mountaineering skills—or at least a boost from a step stool. And it's a long way down.

Left: For a teenage girl, "sweet dreams" means a Scandinavian cupboard bed decorated in the vivid blue and yellow of the Swedish flag. The nook is flanked by spacious closets the depth of the bed, and underneath is a trundle bed for sleepovers.

You can lower an adult-size bed to kid-friendly height by eliminating the box spring. Rest the mattress instead on slats, or on slats topped with a thin board called a "bunkie" (because it's commonly used with bunk beds), available where mattresses are sold. A bed without a box spring has a contemporary "platform" look.

There's a style of bed to make your child's sweet dreams come true.

If you use the mattress solo, select a thick one to give good support and to look proportionate to the bed frame. Your child's age, personal preference, physical needs, and the bed itself will help determine the best configuration. Regardless of setup, choose a quality mattress. Kids may not weigh as much as adults, but they require the same good sleep support.

Top right: Gauzy fabric hanging from bamboo rods (found at a garden shop) gives this sleigh bed a lazy tropical feel.

Bottom right: A hand-painted fantasy garden gives this young girl's bedroom a serene, fairy-tale sense of place. The wispy draped-fabric canopy falls from a decorative wrought-iron ring.

Facing page: An awning canopy that hangs high up on a vibrantly striped wall defines the sleeping area without having any physical connection to the bed itself. This room's decor avoids gender cliches or anything babyish and can grow up with the child who lives here.

An enclosure of some form creates sleeping quarters that kids will love to climb into and will remember forever.

Right: An architect father designed beds for his kids with curtains they can pull closed at bedtime to create a cozy oasis in a warehouse-size room (top photo). The bunk beds occupy an elevated loft space, fenced off with yellow industrial screening. Downstairs is any kid's perfect playroom, with its expanse of hardwood floor from an old gymnasium, multiple activity areas, and plenty of natural light from glass-block walls. Locker-style storage units in playful pink (see detail above) are fun alternatives to conventional shelves.

Right: This is a dream of a bed for a little girl who loves riding horses, playing dress-up, and the color pink. The steeds atop the bedposts, a pullout trundle mattress, and daisy-dotted panels are custom details ordered with the bed. The room's mural fittingly depicts a castle (see below).

Right: A twin-over-full setup is an option for an older kid who feels cramped in a narrow bunk bed yet still wants to host sleepovers. The beds come apart into two freestanding units, so eventually the larger one might even move to a first apartment, with the twin left for a sibling or a guest room.

Facing page: The little princess who lives here has a fairy grandmother with almost magical sewing skills. She constructed the canopy out of exquisite silk fabrics too fragile to use as a bed covering for an active child. (The ready-made comforter cover is durable enough to jump on.) The walls were hand-striped to match the dust ruffle.

Bedding Down
...or Up

**LOFT BED
WITH DESK**

Loft systems

Elevated beds multiply floor space in a bedroom. Styles range from a bed with built-in desk below plus open space for a freestanding bookcase or dresser to configurations that include integral storage—shelves, drawers, and cupboard. Access to the bed is usually via a ladder. Adding a second bed under the loft in an "L" configuration accommodates sleepovers. Include fun accessories like an exit slide and a tent and your kids may never want to leave their room.

Kids spend a lot of time sleeping, so it's important to provide a safe, comfortable sleep surface that supports their growing bodies. Remember, too, that a bed is more to a child than a place to crawl into nightly. It functions early on as a playground, later as a hangout. Choose a bed carefully.

Headboards and footboards

A bed becomes a focal point in the room when you add a headboard, with or without a matching footboard and side rails. A headboard can also provide back support for reading, and it allows placement of the bed away from a wall or angled out from a corner. With built-in shelves or cubbies, a headboard can hold a bedside light, clock, and books.

**TWIN BED
WITH PULLOUT
STORAGE**

Trundle beds

Occupying the same amount of floor space as a twin bed, the trundle is two beds in one: a second mattress pulls out from underneath the main one. Some styles also have built-in drawers between the top mattress and the pullout platform, convenient for storing bedding, pajamas, and toys. Look for trundle options for bunk beds, captain's beds (see below), and standard headboard or headboard–footboard units.

Captain's beds

This bed with built-in storage takes its name from the compact units favored by ships' captains. Sleeping higher than a standard bed but lower than a loft bed, a captain's bed leaves room for storage underneath. Two drawers are common, but some styles offer more elaborate configurations, from shallow cabinets to sets of drawers, an integral desk, a trundle mattress, and more.

TRUNDLE BED

THREE-DRAWER CAPTAIN'S BED

Canopy beds

With an attached overhead framework and often a rooflike covering, canopy beds speak to a girl's inner princess. You can also create a canopy for a standard bed: secure a custom or ready-made frame to the wall high above the headboard or to the ceiling and drape it in gauzy fishnet or swoops of fabric. Versions are also available for four-posters. Look for canopy kits at home furnishings stores or sewing centers.

Keep in mind that sumptuous canopies, like elaborate window treatments, can be elegant dust collectors. They require frequent vacuuming to stay pristine. Simpler versions—such as hanging panels or netting that you can easily remove to clean—set a dreamy scene but are easier to maintain.

CUSTOM WALL-MOUNTED CANOPIES

FOUR-POSTER CANOPY BED

Fantasy beds

Whimsical beds in the form of racing cars, airplanes, and boats are the Rolls-Royces of slumber. They're charming, frequently custom, and often costly. An alternative is a standard twin bed transformed with a fantasy facade bolted to its frame. Such a facade can be removed when the child tires of castles and takes up trains. If you're handy, you can make the facade yourself out of plywood, then paint it or cover it with fabric. Or simply create a fantasy theme with bedding, pictures, and accessories.

Daybeds

Is it a bed or a sofa? A daybed is both. Its high frame stretches along one long side and wraps around the ends into sofa-like arms, marrying the lounging potential of a couch with the comfort of a standard-size twin bed. Kids love this chameleon quality—grown-up sofa by day, cozy bed by night. Some styles include pullout trundle platforms beneath the main mattress for overnight guests.

LOCOMOTIVE BED

DAYBED WITH CANOPY

TUCKED IN
for the Night

Bedding for kids' rooms is no longer an afterthought, destined for obscurity under a bedspread. The selection today is huge, with ever more stores, catalogs, and online sites offering juvenile bedding lines. In fact, bedding for kids now encompasses complete collections: sheets, pillowcases, blankets, and comforters, plus coordinating lamps, rugs, pictures, curtain panels, and throw pillows.

With so many choices, bedding is often the jumping-off point for planning the whole room. An affordable splurge, it's the easiest way to give a room new personality. Transforming a room by swapping superhero sheets for ones populated with space monsters is kinder to a budget than replacing the bed itself.

Kids' bedding comes in fabrics ranging from familiar cotton and blends to cozy flannel or jersey knit as soft as an old T-shirt. You can choose classic gingham checks in fresh hues, vintage florals, or cool surfer stripes in colors that pop.

Basic bedding for kids includes a washable mattress pad, sheets and pillowcases (consider optional decorative shams if your child likes an extra pillow for reading in bed), and a blanket, comforter, or quilt. It's up to you and your child how these elements come together—particularly whether a top sheet is used and whether a comforter takes the place of a blanket. Using a comforter with a removable, washable cover instead of a separate top sheet might encourage kids to make their beds.

Below, right: In the latest colors and patterns, new bedding will transform a child's room without requiring a total makeover.

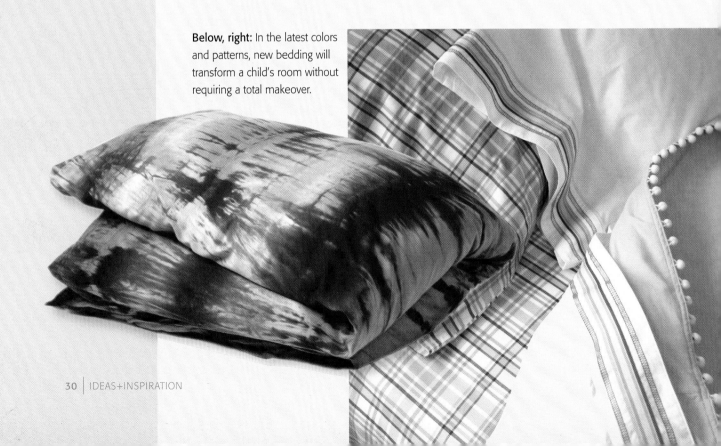

Right: Two pillows offer extra comfort for lounging. A sham that coordinates with a blanket or top sheet polishes the look.

Above: Straighten the quilt and stack the pillows, and this bed is made. Lively bedding fabrics update an heirloom bed for the current generation.

Right: Smoothing out a comforter at night and folding it neatly in the morning is an easy task that even little kids can handle.

Desk Set *Strategies*

AS YOUR CHILD'S WORK SURFACE, do you picture a traditional desk, a sleek cantilevered shelf, or even a simple table? Whether you opt for a brand-new desk right out of the box, a vintage flea-market find, or an unfinished piece transformed with a bright wash of color, make durability and comfort your priorities—especially as homework escalates in the upper grades.

Left: In this study area, with its adjustable acrylic shelves, space was made for work, play, and display.

Ideally, you want a super-size surface that accommodates lighting, reference materials, personal treasures, and collectibles as well as computer and audio components—with plenty of open space for writing and working on projects. Whether there's room for such an imposing piece of furniture is the reality check. But as you'll see on these pages, you can devise appealing work spaces even with limited floor space. What all of them have in common is a look that's practical, high-spirited, and attuned to the room decor.

One solution: divide up activity areas. Nominate a small desk for the computer if the child has one, and dedicate a table elsewhere in the room for reading, games, and creative pursuits. Many families share a computer in the central part of the house, freeing up kids' desks for other activities. Another fix for a space crunch: clear off the desktop. Eliminate clutter by providing shelves, containers, and bins near the desk for books and supplies.

If two kids share a room, ensure peace and privacy with two desks, even if they sit side by side or are located in a quiet hallway. But take study habits into account. If one sister prefers a desk for homework while the other finds inspiration sprawled on the floor or across a bed, one desk is all the room needs.

An adult-size desk becomes a necessity, not an option, when homework starts to pile up.

Wait until your child is 10 or older to invest in an adult-size desk. That's usually when homework begins to pile up and a desk becomes a necessity, not an option. The bigger the better, say many parents. Kids have projects beyond schoolwork involving crafts, art, or hobbies, and they need room to spread out. On the other hand, a more modest desk will do if you or your kids are big fans of the kitchen table as the spot for family activities.

Top right: When two kids share desk duty, assigned seats and designated drawers head off squabbles. Desktop initials mark off territory on the work surface.

Bottom right: Offering plenty of storage, a classic student's desk is hardworking and built to last. Its honey-toned hardwood warms up the room decor.

Facing page: As part of a handsome loft system, this space-saving desk with corkboard merges seamlessly with bunk beds, all constructed of warm-hued wood. The gooseneck study lamp doubles as a light for reading in bed.

Right: Children's bedrooms become true havens for relaxing and socializing when desks are elsewhere. These side-by-side workstations are set up in the den to create a homework center for two siblings. Kid-friendly details include cork message boards, a durable striped laminate floor, and supportive swivel chairs.

Above: Display boards and colorful collectibles give personality to a small but functional study area.

Right: Sun-saturated colors rejuvenate a secondhand desk and chair. Both were stripped of their old finish and painted with glossy, heavy-duty enamel—hot pink for the desk, tropical orange for the chair. High-gloss paint not only looks great, it wipes clean with mild soap and water.

Below: The preteen who lives here divides and conquers when it comes to homework. Rather than using a single large surface, she assigns one area for computer work and another for other projects.

Above: There wasn't room on this teen's desk for a computer and printer. To accommodate both, a cabinetmaker constructed a separate return that forms an "L" with the desk. The two pieces blend because both share the same leg style and shiny white finish. A pullout keyboard tray stores under the new work surface.

Above: Ideas must flow for the student who sits at this magical desk, crafted by his furniture-designer father. Simple in style yet charming in detail, it would doubtless inspire creativity even if it faced a blank wall.

Above: Nearby storage keeps this desk uncluttered and ready for the day's homework assignments. A display board fills an underutilized space above the work surface. Hanging shelves store supplies, reference materials, and CDs off the desktop but within easy reach. Task lighting is recessed below the shelving.

Above: How can two brothers share one workstation? Give each boy a mobile storage unit underneath the desktop. This efficient homework center occupies a converted closet.

Facing page: Metal bins keep things neat on a modern desk with multiple shelves but no drawers. With its clean lines and simple construction, this desk will prove useful even after the child moves out—assuming he doesn't take it with him.

Desks
and Tables

NIGHTSTAND

ROLLING STORAGE TABLE

OCCASIONAL TABLE

Kids need a place for a lamp and an alarm clock, homework, games, and music— or just a solid spot to prop their elbows and daydream. No matter what kind of desk or table you choose to satisfy this need, make sure it is well constructed and doesn't have any sharp or protruding edges. Easy-to-maintain surfaces are important. If there are drawers, check that they glide smoothly and safely.

Desks

Select a desk that offers long-term usefulness. Even younger school-age children are savvy about technology, and standard computers and CD players require a full-size desk to support them. Many types of desks are available in a wide range of prices. Most are freestanding, but you can also find them incorporated into bunk and loft structures. A long built-in shelf along one wall or straddling a corner makes a sleek and space-efficient desk. Desks with hutch units keep supplies organized and within easy reach.

You can also configure a desk from purchased components: home centers and some furniture retailers offer finished tops and legs in a range of sizes, colors, and styles. Or simply rest a work surface on a pair of file cabinets, a functional setup that will last beyond the teen years.

A computer desk usually features shelves and ledges for components. A regular desk can be made more computer-friendly by attaching

PLAY TABLE AND CHAIRS

CHILD'S SET WITH CHALKBOARD SURFACE

a keyboard tray to its underside and adding a platform for the monitor on the desktop surface. Look for accessories at places that sell computers or office furniture. If your child uses a laptop, it can sit right on the desk. Whatever arrangement you use, make sure either the desktop or the chair can be adjusted so that the child's forearms are parallel with the floor, with elbows slightly higher than the keyboard.

SIDE-BY-SIDE DESKS

DESK WITH
HUTCH UNIT

Bedside tables

Turn out the light? Turn off the alarm? A night table lets kids do both from the comfort of their beds. It's a must unless the headboard has built-in storage. Most furniture collections include storage units specifically designed as bedside tables, with open and closed storage areas. But a low bookcase or occasional table can serve just as well. Just be sure your child can reach the top surface easily from bed.

Pint-size furniture

Little kids love furniture that's just their size. It gives them a sense of control in a world furnished for Gullivers. A diminutive table is a functional purchase for kids up to age six. The safest ones have smooth, rounded edges and legs that splay out for stability. They'll get a workout, so get one that's extra sturdy. You want easy cleanup, too; look for a table with a washable finish.

If you purchase a set, the chairs will be scaled to the height of the companion table. If you buy chairs separately, check that they're a good fit to the table you pair them with. Or use backless stools—small fry often work leaning forward.

Chairs
and Fun Seating

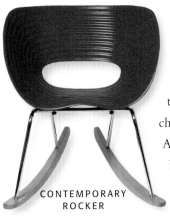

CONTEMPORARY ROCKER

Provide kids with at least two types of seating to meet their needs, which can change from day to day. A casual place to sit can be a beanbag, the bed, or even a carpet. For schoolwork, kids need a stable, support- ive desk chair. If there's room, a cozy spot for reading is a third option.

Let your child test out any chair for comfort before you bring it home.

Desk chairs

To sit through—and finish—hours of home- work, kids need chairs with good back support and overall comfort. Office-style chairs with ergonomic features like adjustable backs and seats are the most versatile. Chairs that swivel or move on casters give quick access to nearby storage. On the other hand, zooming around on casters could mar floors and dent baseboards. And some kids prefer swiveling to studying; keep that in mind if your child is easily distracted.

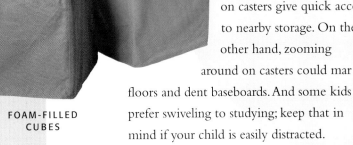

FOAM-FILLED CUBES

Straight-back chairs with four legs offer stable seating. You can choose classic styles in wood or colorful modern versions with tubular frames and molded backs.

For younger kids, select a desk chair that is sturdy but not too hefty for them to move.

For easy comfort

An easy chair isn't a must in a kid's room. But if you have room for one, it offers special comforts. For little ones, it's a special spot for parent-child reading sessions. For older kids, it serves as a retreat for reading and day- dreaming, as seating for friends, or perhaps even as an extra bed for guests (some chairs convert into sleeping space).

An adult-size chair has staying power beyond the teen years, but expect little kids to find it cozy only when shared with a grown-up. They're happier in chairs their own size; lots of these are available in fun styles, playful fabrics, and bright finishes. There's no rush, though, to buy a reading chair—requests for a place to read other than the bed usually don't start until about age 13 or 14.

LOUNGING PILLOWS

INFLATABLE
ARMCHAIR

EASY CHAIR
AND
OTTOMAN

Squishy seating

What kid wouldn't like to sink into
seating that's as cushy as a cloud?
Children love soft, comfortable places
for their bodies. When it's all about
comfort, indulge your child with
practical, casual seating in the form of
a beanbag, a funky inflatable chair, or
anything foam-filled.

If you've only a sliver of space, not
enough for a soft chair, go mobile;
scatter a pile of big pillows on the
floor or fill an empty corner with a
plump ottoman. A child can move
these around easily and then later
store them out of the way.

BEANBAG
CHAIR

MODULAR
CHAISE

SWIVEL
CHAIR WITH
CASTERS

STRAIGHT-
BACKED CHAIR

ROLLING
TRACTOR SEAT

43

Color with Kids
in Mind

WATERMELON PINK. JUICY ORANGE. True blue. When it comes to choosing the colors for a kid's room, it's not just pastels or primaries anymore. As you plan the room's scheme, take your cue from your children and their world. Anything goes for inspiration—from a bag of jelly beans to a tank of tropical fish to the regalia of your child's favorite sports team.

Let kids know if the colors in their room must tie in with what's already in the home. If so, then you have an obvious starting point. If not, get inspiration from the ready-made palettes all around you. Browse kids' clothing departments, bedding displays, fabric shops, toy stores, and poster shops for color combinations that look fresh and fun but also have staying power. Magazines and catalogs are another great resource.

Color is an easy way for siblings to give their rooms unique personality. Does one child thrive in an energized environment? Consider a scheme of lemonade yellow and tractor red. Is the other more at home in a serene retreat? A tranquil oasis in soft blues and greens could be just right.

Left: The color red on the daybed frame, the accent pillows, and the matting for the framed drawings unifies a preteen's laid-back space.

Tips about color

Young kids tend to prefer bright, energizing hues. Use these as accents, balanced with more soothing colors. Extended colors—those to which a little black, white, or gray has been added—are softer and more complex; they suit all ages, including teens. They're pleasing to live with, too, for parents who cringe at crayon brights. Here are some more ways to make color work for you:

▪ Use color to highlight architectural features or unify disparate elements in a room. Visually enlarge a small, busy room by painting all features— walls, moldings, windows, and doors—the same color.

▪ Make a room feel cozier with warm and dark colors, which seem to advance visually. Cool and light colors, which recede, appear to enlarge a room. Lift a low ceiling by painting it a pale, cool hue. To make a tall space more intimate, paint the ceiling a dark, warm tone.

▪ Use colors in unequal amounts. Let one color star, and delegate two or three other hues to supporting roles in the room decor.

▪ Use low-intensity colors in large amounts, more intense colors in smaller areas.

▪ Use a color more than once or it will look out of place.

▪ Combine colors of similar value— all light, all dark. Or combine colors of similar intensities—all bright, all subtle. Avoid monotony by adding a few dark colors to a light scheme or a shot of intense color to a quiet scheme.

Above: Vivid, kid-pleasing colors are a perfect backdrop for game-board graphics. Even the closet gets a color makeover in deep pink.

Right: The colors of a favorite college football team inspired a sports-minded seven-year-old to root for a red-and-black room. Fabric panels are attached with self-fastening strips to L-shaped wood supports that are screwed to the ceiling.

Facing page: Bold colors work well in the room pictured on these two pages thanks to their varied intensities and values. Green is such a universal favorite that it is sometimes referred to as the "fourth primary." Here it complements the cardinal red of the four-poster bed and harmonizes with the draperies and storage piece.

Left: Painting this tall chest the same color as the wall makes it recede, a designer's trick for visually opening up a room. The deep blue-violet of the beanbag chair adds a fresh accent.

Below: The splash of ruby red and lipstick pink on the two chairs balances the room's cool shades and pumps up the volume. The plush upholstered piece at left is a family heirloom passed down from a great-great-grandmother.

Above: Against a green wall, this lavender floor-to-ceiling storage unit is a standout. Its school-inspired cubbies contain the clutter and make cleanup a cinch. The lower shelves offer easy access to a young child, while house rules dictate that parents retrieve stuff from higher up. The piece is bolted in place for stability.

Facing page: A playful, colorful circus-tent canopy that originally hung over the child's crib adapts perfectly to a more grownup space. The occupant is lucky to have a designer mom who knows treasure from trash at the flea market—all the furnishings are vintage, including the old patio set shown in the photo above. In a former life, this sofa was aging outdoor furniture. It was revived with new striped cushions and a powder-coated finish in taxi yellow. The circus prints come from a vintage "Bozo the Clown" record album.

Left: Purple, green, and blue are the signature colors of the girl who lives here, and she wanted them everywhere in her room. Her interior-designer mother suggested painting two opposite walls greenish yellow, the other two aqua. Deep purple—on cornice, ottoman, and headboard—anchors the lighter shades. The bedding completes the soothing yet sophisticated palette. The walls are glazed, a decorative finish that gives depth and transparency to paint.

Window *Dressing*

When thinking about how to dress a window, be guided first and foremost by a child's need for light control. Consider yourself lucky if your kids can doze off with midsummer sunlight still streaming into their room come bedtime. Most children require window treatments that either dim the light or block it entirely. For very young children, keep safety considerations in mind (see page 117).

Curtains and draperies

From breezy sheers to whimsical polka-dot panels, curtains add color and soften the hard edges of a child's room. Depending on the fabric, curtains can filter light or block it entirely and provide partial or complete privacy. Layering curtain panels—heavier over sheer—is one attractive option for light control. Even more effective are curtains paired with blinds or blackout shades.

There's no trick to installing curtains: simply gather them on the rod or attach them to the rod with rings or tabs. And today's curtain hardware is as decorative as the fabric itself. Tiebacks shaped like stars or butterflies—or rods capped with vintage airplanes or sparkly beaded balls—have great kid appeal.

More formal than curtains, draperies hang in pleats and elegant folds that definitely dress up a window. Paired with coordinating wallpaper and bedding, they give a room a polished look. If your child needs to sleep in total darkness, line the draperies with blackout material.

Blinds and shutters

With their rotating slats, blinds and shutters offer optimal light control as well as total privacy. They're also relatively easy to clean. Blinds are available in wood or metal, with 1- to 3-inch-wide slats and great choices in color and trim. Handsome wooden blinds are a less expensive shutter substitute.

As a classic treatment that enhances any decor, shutters are peerless. Stock shutters are sold at home centers at a fraction of the price of custom shutters, though their less-sturdy construction means they may not last as long—especially around energetic kids.

Wide slats—whether on blinds or shutters—look best for large windows.

DENIM VALANCE

Shades

Nice to look at and simple to operate, shades control light, insulate the window, and offer privacy. Use them alone or team them with curtains, draperies, or valances.

Roller shades offer a clean look at a reasonable cost. Find them in smart new fabrics and decorator hues, with whimsical trims, hems, and pulls. For privacy below and light above, consider roller styles that pull up from the sill.

ROMAN SHADE

Soft shades present an uncluttered look. Roman styles draw up into crisp or softly rounded horizontal folds. Dressier balloon shades have airy, rounded poufs. Insulating cellular shades, with honeycomb pockets, keep kids' rooms cool in summer, cozy in winter.

Room-darkening shades have a special lining that totally blocks out light for kids who require it.

WOODEN BLINDS

FABRIC SHADE WITH FIXED CURTAIN

Flooring That's *Kid-Proof*

THROW RUG

If you think of flooring in a child's room as furniture, selecting the right type becomes easier. At any given time, the floor functions as chair, table, or bed as well as a surface on which to walk. Choose a flooring material that supports the gamut of kids' activities, doesn't show every scuff and stain, and cleans up easily.

Resilient surfaces

Malleable flooring materials—linoleum, vinyl, cork, and rubber—share the virtue of comfort underfoot. Improved protective finishes help further kid-proof a category of flooring already long appreciated as hard-wearing and easy to maintain. Resilients provide a flat surface for play and are moisture and stain resistant. Costs are moderate, though they increase for custom or imported products or for professional installation.

Retro linoleum is a comeback kid for its new palette of bright colors and its natural composition—it's an eco-friendly material made of

CORK

linseed oil, ground cork, and wood flour. Ever-popular vinyl is available in countless colors, patterns, textures, and styles that invite creative combinations. Cushy cork is a warm, natural touch that also mutes playful shrieks, footsteps, and the "clunk" of dropped toys. Another sound-absorbent surface, rugged rubber flooring offers skid-proof footing for active kids and a adds contemporary accent to their rooms.

Versatile laminate, a relative newcomer in flooring, sandwiches a photograph of a natural material—many patterns emulate wood—between a protective wear coat and a sturdy core. This easy-to-maintain surface looks great and is quick to install. You almost can't abuse it; today's laminate amazingly resists dents, burns, and stains.

LINOLEUM

Resilients are relatively soft, making them vulnerable to dents and tears. Head off problems by using floor protectors under furniture legs, and cover glides with felt pads. Sweep or vacuum the floor regularly and mop up dirt.

Wood floors

A wood floor has almost all the features any parent (and kid) could want: a natural beauty and warm appearance, relatively minimal care requirements, and a smooth surface that supports pint-size construction projects. It can be restored with refinishing, so you can expect it to last a lifetime.

The cost for a material with all these advantages, however, will be moderate to high, depending on the wood selection and finish. And a bare wood floor can be noisy—and hard on bottoms. Keep in mind that hardwoods like oak are less likely to be dented by a dropped toy than softwoods like fir or pine.

CUSTOM RESILIENT FLOOR

HAND-STENCILED HARDWOOD FLOOR

TEXTURED RUBBER

Area rugs

Scatter area rugs and smaller throw rugs over a bare floor to absorb sound as well as to provide cushioned seating and warmth underfoot. They're a great, easily changeable way to incorporate a child's favorite color. Especially for younger kids, leave plenty of open space around these cozy islands for racing cars or playing games.

Look for old-fashioned hooked rugs and braided ovals in soft fibers and wonderful colors, low-pile loop rugs in bright tones and fun shapes, and super-shaggy styles for teens. The most practical throw rugs have nonskid backings. Anchor larger area rugs with rug pads, which also protect the floor beneath. Prices vary widely, depending on style, size, material, and construction.

CUT-PILE RUGS

BRAIDED RUG

LOW-PILE LOOP RUGS

Carpet

A carpet muffles footsteps, keeps toes warm on cold mornings, and cushions falls. Wall-to-wall carpeting is a good choice for all but the very young or the very messy (often the same).

Choose a low pile for kids' rooms— it's fairly flat, a good surface for play. Don't expect kids to treat their carpet with respect; pick a fiber that is both stain and soil resistant, with good resiliency. Easy-care nylon is a popular choice, as is more costly wool.

SHORT-LOOP CARPETING

Use a thick, soft padding for comfort, longer carpet life, and improved insulation as well as protection for the floor. Frequent vacuuming will extend carpet life and improve air quality in the room. You'll find a selection of carpeting in every price category. Ask if the price includes padding and installation, and removal of any old carpeting.

WALL-TO-WALL NEEDLEPOINT CARPETING

ROOM-SIZE HOOKED RUG

Artful Ways
with Paint

APPLIED INVENTIVELY, a punch of fresh paint transforms even the plainest of rooms into a memorable child's space. Wall motifs ranging from playful stripes to beloved storybook creatures can add visual impact or establish a theme. Brush on a little surface charm to basic furnishings like dressers and armoires, and you've converted ho-hum pieces into real attention-getters.

Is an elaborate design or scene what you and your child have in mind? Unless you're a confident Picasso, you'll probably want to hire a muralist. According to decorative painters, murals are most popular with younger kids. By about age 10, kids develop strong opinions about how they want their surroundings to look. They—and their walls—will be ready for a change.

Installing a mural can be expensive—and who wouldn't hesitate before painting over a mural when a room is set for a face-lift? Muralists offer some tips for expanding the life of a fantasy finish. Avoid babyish subjects and the scene will be appreciated longer. Select a classic theme: nature, sports, animals, or a pattern that has staying power; the hero of the moment does not. Use sophisticated colors rather than pastels or trendy hues. Finally, if a room has a mural and its occupant

Left: The Old West is an obvious theme for a young Texan. The painted walls are stamped with brands designed from family initials.

is lobbying for a new look, don't change the mural—change the kid. Ask her to swap spaces with a younger sibling. If the theme is gender neutral, the mural will delight a younger brother as much as it did his big sis.

Above all, remember whose room this is. When it comes to walls, there needs to be more to surface finishes than meets the eye. The goal is to make them kid-friendly as well as great looking. That means selecting paints or surface treatments that are both durable and easy to clean.

A punch of paint transforms even the plainest of rooms into a memorable child's space.

Top right: With their magnificently rendered magical creatures, the walls of this room seem like pages from a storybook. Using blue and white in a bedroom creates a serene yet fresh mood that is perfect for a child.

Bottom right: Framed by an arch, a mural opens up the room so that it seems to flow onto an enchanting terrace overlooking a sparkling lake.

Below: Their room may be in a high-rise apartment, but to the city kids who live here, their home is their castle. Like a stage set, the walls are transformed with paint into fortified towers, with a knight on horseback in the distance. Multicolor pendants resembling heraldic flags hang at the window.

Left: A charming faux headboard painted on the wall gives a plain twin bed the Cinderella treatment.

Above: Old-fashioned yet sophisticated colors create a magical mood for a girls' room. The blue of the walls is a pleasing, noncompeting backdrop for the room's many shades of green. Hand-painted stripes set off the antique shutters, which fold and unfold on piano hinges for light control.

Right: To create this cheerful, feminine design over yellow walls, the muralist marked repeats at chair rail and ceiling as a guide, then defined the diamond pattern by "connecting the dots" with charcoal (easily brushed away). The diagonal white stripes and whimsical accents were then applied freehand with acrylic paint.

Right: Into the woods! The decorating plan for this storybook bedroom followed naturally from the hand-painted furniture. The fabric patterns—none of them juvenile prints—combine for a more sophisticated look that will transition well as the child gets older. Glazed walls, a tree mural, and a painted border all contribute charm. A high-rise gazebo in the form of a tiny tea shop attaches to the wall as if resting in the limbs of the mural tree (see detail above).

FUN EFFECTS
with Special Paints

For a quick room fix, try a specialty paint to supply funky fun. All the following paints are easy to apply and can be found at paint stores, hardware stores, and home centers.

With *chalkboard paint,* the writing's on the wall (or floor or furniture)—and that's okay! Paint the lower half of a wall to create a chalkboard wainscot, trimmed with picture molding to hold chalk. Paint a closet door, the drawer fronts of a dresser, or the wall space above a desk. Create a chalkboard square on the floor for sidewalk artists. Chalkboard paint is available in black or green, either in liquid form to brush or roll on or as an aerosol spray.

Battleship-gray *magnetic paint* contains bits of metal that create magnet-friendly spaces for displaying important stuff, from posters to game tickets to school assignments. Unless you like its somber shade, you can paint over it with regular interior paint or chalkboard paint without losing its magnetic properties.

Glitter paint is like pixie dust to little kids, or a touch of Hollywood glamour for preteens. Multicolored glitter is suspended in a clear coat that you apply over regular wall paint. The chameleon-like glitter takes on whatever color it covers, giving pizzazz to walls or furniture.

Use *glow-in-the-dark paint* to create shimmering stars and planets on your child's ceiling. The paint brightens in intensity in dark or dim rooms, glowing for about 30 minutes after the lights go out—just long enough for a little one who's afraid of the dark to fall asleep. The paint is a faint phosphorescent green when the room is light, like an illuminated watch dial.

Below: The black closet door is also a writing surface. It's sealed with several coats of chalkboard paint.

Above: Bugs, butterflies, and growing things of all kinds appeal to a broad age group and are gender neutral. The hand-painted panels of the armoire shown above and the mini–woodland scene on the ottoman at top are like windows that let you peek into a magic garden. Hand-rendered stripes give personality to companion pieces.

Top right: Keeping this room neat should be a slam-dunk. A large closet hides behind a mural lifted from a sports training room. Their paneled facade gives the faux lockers an added sense of dimension.

Bottom right: A bunkhouse bedroom houses three brothers in fine Western style, right up to the log walls painted by the boys' clever mother. The curtains were created from flannel blankets, grommeted and tied to an iron rod with strips of leather.

No snorkel's required to get up close and personal to this marine life. How to make a room for two brothers that's exciting to be in yet restful come bedtime? Transform it into an aquarium. Furnishings are minimized to focus attention on the finny swimmers on the walls, and toys are stored elsewhere in the house.

Wall *Finishes*

PEEL-OFF WALL
APPLIQUES

A child's room is the perfect blank canvas for paint or wallpaper. Apply paint in bold swaths of color, as a fanciful mural, or as whimsical stenciled or stamped patterns. Make an impact with wallpaper, an easy way to set a theme, perk up a room devoid of architectural interest, or visually correct a room's flaws. Or devise a surface finish that's as unique as your child, like the climbing wall pictured on the facing page.

Paint

Choosing the color isn't the only decision you need to make about paint. You must also decide on the finish and type.

A water-base (latex) paint in a wipable low-luster finish is a popular choice for kids' walls, partnered with a durable, washable semigloss finish for trim. Water-base paints are nearly odorless, easy to apply, and quick to dry. Oil-base paints have solvents that make them very durable but also very smelly, slow to dry, and a nuisance to clean up.

A new generation of water-base enamel paints performs nearly as well as their oil-base counterparts, with fewer toxic solvents. Also check out health- and environment-friendly paints with low or no VOCs (volatile organic compounds), containing fewer solvents and giving off less odor (see 113).

A visit to a paint store will help clarify which paint type will best suit your project. In any case, keep a freshly painted child's room well ventilated—open the windows and turn on a fan—to reduce exposure to toxic fumes.

Wallpaper

If wallpaper is to be the backdrop, bring paint chips, fabric swatches, and color illustrations to the wallpaper store to guide you. On the other hand, a preliminary shopping visit might just turn up a wallpaper pattern that inspires the room's whole decor, or a border that makes plain walls pop. Either way, to estimate how much paper to order, have room dimensions with you, as well as window sizes and door placements.

WALLPAPER WITH BORDER TRIM

HAND-LETTERED STORYBOOK MOTIF

Save delicate textures and fragile materials for other rooms. Vinyl wallpaper and kids are meant for each other: vinyl is the sturdiest paper and the easiest to install. Also decide which of these features are most important to you, then ask to see papers that have them:

- Scrubbable—cleans with a brush or detergent
- Washable—cleans with occasional soap-and-water sponging
- Stain-resistant—stains can be thoroughly removed
- Abrasion-resistant—withstands scraping and rubbing
- Colorfast—won't fade in sunlight
- Prepasted—apply water and it's ready to hang
- Peelable—pattern can be peeled, but backing will remain (fine if wallpaper is a long-term choice)
- Strippable—paper can be dry-peeled, leaving little paste or adhesive residue

TEXTURED STUCCO CLIMBING WALL

PAINTED WALL WITH FLORAL TREATMENT

Bright Ideas
for Lighting

Good lighting enhances decor and supports the activities that take place in a room. As children work, play, and lounge within the four walls of their bedroom, they need a lighting scheme that is multifunctional. That means you'll need to provide them with more than just one light fixture.

FANTASY WALL FIXTURE

Ceiling fixtures

An overhead fixture supplies general illumination that allows a child to safely navigate around the room, play on the floor, or draw at an easel. Its ambient glow makes the room less scary for little ones and more inviting for kids of any age.

Ceiling fixtures are anything but boring these days. You'll find shades with star cutouts and tea-party chandeliers, lanterns in soft or vivid hues, and futuristic multi-armed pendants. Track fixtures are versatile and easy to install, accepting both low-voltage and standard lights. And what teen wouldn't love a ceiling fan/light combination?

CEILING LAMP

Wall fixtures

Wall-mounted lamps can provide localized task lighting for reading or, if they're mostly decorative, throw a soft and pleasing indirect light. Fixtures that are hard-wired to the wall eliminate loose cords. If that's not possible, surface-mount the fixture and plug it into a nearby outlet. For safety and neatness, hide cords behind heavy furniture or secure them in covers attached to the wall.

Since young kids can't tip them over, wall fixtures can be safer than table lamps—unless your child is an agile climber.

WALL-MOUNTED LAMPS

Freestanding lamps

Set on a chest or on a table next to the bed, a table lamp casts a cozy pool of light. Today's lamps for kids are especially decorative; many are designed as part of bedding collections, with shades and bases that mix and match.

Choose a lamp that's weighted so it doesn't tip over easily. For very young kids, consider securing the lamp base to the furniture. Floor lamps are best to reserve for older kids who aren't likely to knock them over.

Task lamps, which often have adjustable necks, supply a focused beam for reading, working on art projects, or doing schoolwork. Easily adjusted clip-on lights supply practical task lighting for a headboard, an upper bunk bed, or a crowded desk. Clipped to a shelf, they're also a great way to light up a collection. Check that their grip is secure.

Night-lights

Plug-in, low-wattage night-lights chase away the monsters. Some automatically glow when a room is dark, while others have to be switched on. Choices are endless and styles so appealing that you might come home with one for yourself as well. Locate a night-light away from any flammable materials.

Novelty lights

Just for fun, brighten a wall with a string of lights in fantasy shapes. Preschoolers to teens adore them, and new designs keep popping up all the time. Corral a herd of home-on-the-range horses for a young cowboy or equestrienne. Drape a preteen's mirror with exotic paper lanterns. Flexible rope lights with tiny bulbs encased in plastic tubes light up the night like fireflies.

NIGHT-LIGHTS

ADJUSTABLE TASK LAMP

CLIP-ON LAMP

CANDLESTICK-STYLE FLOOR LAMP

Two (or More)
Is Company

DESIGNING A ROOM to be shared by siblings is a challenge many parents face. A shared room must meet the needs of each of its residents for space, individuality, and privacy. And even if the room has only one regular occupant, you'd be wise to plan for overnight guests. That way, you won't throw the room into a shambles every time you put up a visitor.

Children are a lot more flexible about sharing a room than we give them credit for. In fact, many kids enjoy the company. But it's inevitable that they'll get on each other's nerves now and then. Here are some ideas to help you make the best of togetherness.

A symmetrical arrangement of furnishings can keep the peace between siblings. It also creates a serene mood in an often-crowded room, as will personal space that is equally divided and well defined. Visibly mark territory with color or personalized accessories. Or enlist your kids to devise an unobtrusive "mine and yours" system. This can be as simple as assigning everything on the right—right bed, right bank of drawers, right side of the closet—to one child, everything on the left to the other.

Arrange sleeping quarters to maximize privacy. Try bunk beds (if siblings can agree on who sleeps where), removing occupants from

Left: All the elements of this cheerful space down to the bedding were inherited when a big sister redid her room, proof that good design lasts.

each other's view at night, or place twin beds at right angles with a table between. Physical dividers—from a built-in partition to hospital-style privacy curtains in a breezy fabric, a folding screen, or a two-sided shelving unit—clearly define personal space. Allocate space fairly: try to divide the room so that each child claims a special feature, such as a window or a niche.

Ignore the rules, if necessary, to make the floor plan work. Angling bunk beds out from a corner or positioning them perpendicular to the center of a wall can divide the room into two intimate spaces, one for each child. Don't be limited by architectural features; interrupt a window with a bed, if necessary, to maximize wall space. A headboard with an open frame will still let in the view.

For sleepovers, you don't necessarily even need two beds. A chair or ottoman that unfolds into a mattress does double duty. A trundle slips out of sight under a twin bed or a lower bunk bed when not in use, freeing floor space.

Top right: This modular system is both captain's quarters and entertainment for a young swashbuckler and his crew of friends. The bed's skull-and-crossbones flag inspired the pirate-ship wall mural.

Bottom right: Simple furnishings, few accessories, and soft hues minimize the visual bulk of three beds in one room.

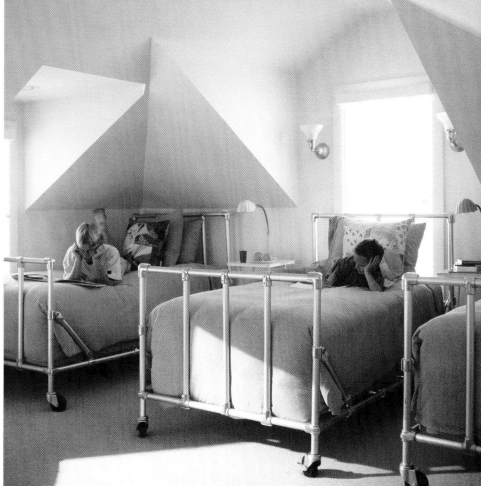

Right, top: Three generations of one family have slept in these charming beds, made elegant with a glossy black finish for their current occupants, two teenage girls. The elder sister chose the black-and-white sunflower fabric as a nine-year-old. It was quite a sophisticated choice for a child, but it proved to be a good one—the girls love it just as much today as they did years ago.

Right, bottom: On sleepover nights, two explorer friends can take a walk on the wild side by climbing into bunk beds made of logs.

Facing page: With a daybed in addition to a regular twin bed, this boy's room is always ready for sleepovers. The space is organized around a set of red-painted furniture that the boy's mother was given as a child. Labeled plastic tubs and deep bookshelves (shown above) make it easy to keep belongings organized and neat.

Below: The challenge was to design a "splashy and fun" room for siblings who once had their own rooms. The centerpiece is a custom shelf unit with a table that detaches and folds up for storage.

Above: How to fit two beds in a room with off-center windows? Break the rules. Place the beds where you want them even if it means that one of the headboards interrupts the view. An antique chest serves as bedside table and storage for both beds.

Left: Despite a five-year age difference, the two sisters who share this room have similar tastes. They both love antiques, furniture made from traditional dark woods, and bold colors. The fabrics, selected first, inspired the raspberry shade on the walls.

Facing page: These pine beds featuring slender pencil posts were made for their teenage owner when she was two years old. The shamrock cutouts in the footboards reflect the family's Irish heritage and also foretold this teen's passion—Irish dancing. Simple sheer panels shirred on rods define the headboard areas. Their decorative tassels repeat the soft green-and-blue color scheme and add polish.

Personal space that is well defined will keep the peace between siblings who share a room.

Top right: With beds this inviting, a room that sleeps three seems cozy, not cramped. An old-fashioned wainscot encircles the walls, tying everything together and providing a handsome architectural backdrop for the furnishings.

Bottom right: Not just any beds would do for an aspiring dancer who needs lots of space for rehearsing, plus room for the occasional overnight guest. Beds with clean, simple lines work best. A wooden handrail attached to a mirrored wall offers support during practice sessions.

BUNK HOUSE
Pointers

Going up? Sleeping above it all affords kids privacy, fun, and a lofty—and empowering—view of a world outfitted for taller folk. Bunk beds are handy for sleepovers and are classic space savers, especially when two kids share a room.

You'll find a bunk style for every room setup, from twin-twin combinations to bunks with a twin on top and a full-size bed on the bottom, and even trundle options that expand sleepover capacity. Typically, the beds stack. But you can also find L-shaped arrangements of freestanding beds. Many bunk sets also reconfigure into separate beds—useful when your child wants to return to ground level, when you want to create a loftlike study or play space beneath the upper bunk, or when you need beds in two different rooms.

Keep in mind that access to the top bunk is limited. Changing sheets can be awkward, and tidying the bedding a daily challenge. On hot nights, the child who sleeps up top could swelter if the room doesn't have good ventilation.

Safety considerations

Hold off on accommodating requests for bunk beds until you decide your child is ready. You can usually rely on preteens—roughly ages 9 to 12—not to fall out of bed or be scared of heights. Kids under age 6 should not sleep in an upper bunk.

When you're shopping for a bunk bed, keep the following safety tips in mind:

- Look for solid construction. Shake the bed. Make sure it doesn't wobble.
- Is there a guardrail on each side of the upper bunk, screwed or bolted to the bed frame? Little kids can roll off the bed and be trapped against the wall. The top of each guardrail should be at least 5 inches above the mattress. So that heads can't squeeze through, be sure the gap between rail slats is no more than 3½ inches.
- Does the mattress correctly fit the bed? You don't want any gaps between mattress and headboard or footboard.
- Can the ladder be secured to the bed frame? You want it steady for climbing.
- Is there adequate headroom between upper and lower beds?

The U.S. Consumer Product Safety Commission has issued a mandatory safety standard for bunk beds—see *www.cpsc.gov* or call (800) 638-2772.

Left: Glossy white bunk beds with blue-striped bedding look crisp and fresh in a house by the shore. Hand-painted details—a nautical motif on the floor, sea shells on the walls—set the theme.

Six years old is considered the minimum safe age for sleeping in an upper bunk. The lower bed is fine for a younger child.

Living Large
in a Small Space

THOUGH SMALL ROOMS are a challenge to furnish, kids find their intimate scale cozy, not confining. The key is to allot the available square footage carefully. Organized properly, it will become the tiny but terrific haven that every child needs. It's critical to keep a small room clutter-free, or your child will feel overwhelmed. Have a dedicated space for everything.

Pare down belongings to essentials—the most-loved toys, books, and collectibles, as well as basic clothing. If possible, store out-of-season or seldom-used gear elsewhere in the house.

Ingenious solutions for space-shy rooms utilize areas that are often overlooked. Hang racks and pegs on closet and entry doors for off-the-floor storage. On the other hand, if opening the closet door takes room you don't have, remove it. Then fill the niche with a dresser or install a ready-to-assemble closet system. Put the underbed wasteland to good use with drawers that roll out or a trundle mattress for sleepovers. Select a headboard that incorporates bookshelves and cubbies without taking up much extra space. Built-ins can be worth the cost when you must shoe-horn in essential furnishings, from a bed to a desk to shelving and drawers.

Left: Even in a small space, there's always room for a retreat beyond the bed. The plush pink chair looks like kids' furniture but is really a scaled-down adult piece discovered at a flea market.

Kids like their belongings to be in plain view. Rather than hiding them all away in the closet, use containers throughout the room to organize toys, books, sporting equipment, and clothes. Encourage children to be neat by providing them with dressers they can reach, a stylish armoire, or catchalls that let them toss things under the bed—and get away with it.

In a small room, have a dedicated space for everything.

Give a small room big style with a simple color scheme that repeats throughout the room. Don't feel restricted to kids' furnishings because of their size—look for small-scale adult pieces that will grow with your child. And don't shy away from the drama of an oversize accessory. A huge mirror, for example, will not only open up the room but also add a touch of whimsy.

Right: This former cottage mudroom has no closets—underbed drawers and a built-in bookcase handle the storage load (top photo). A huge mirror, enclosed in an antique tin frame, seems to expand the diminutive room—a decorator's trick. It also allows a little girl who loves to play dress-up one last look before that curtain call.

Below: To stretch this home's square footage, an unused attic was finished into a cozy girl's bedroom. The low wall resulting from the roofline created a decorating challenge, but a bright color scheme and wallpaper on ceiling and walls make the space feel bigger than it is. Deep recessed drawers maximize an "invisible" space behind the wall (inset photo), expanding the room's storage potential.

Facing page, above: Despite minimal square footage, this room offers a choice of activity areas for the boy who lives here. There's a desk for schoolwork and a stack of floor pillows for hanging out. There's also his grandfather's childhood rocker, rescued from the garage. A baseball painting dominates the sleeping space but seems just right against a backdrop of neutral colors.

Facing page, left: Thanks to a good floor plan, this compact room serves its occupant well. He can sleep, study, play, and entertain pals in his own private space. The daybed is not just for slumber—it's also a comfortable spot for hanging out during the day. Hidden behind a removable bedskirt is a trundle bed for sleepovers. Unifying everything is yellow-and-gold star paper on both the ceiling and the walls.

Below: A shelf unit fitted with colorful plastic bins organizes toys and collections, simplifying cleanup.

Storage *Solutions*

HANGING SHELF

Don't fret if your child's closet space is skimpy. With inventive storage strategies, there can be a sensible spot for everything.

Closets

Do kids need a closet? One with an upper shelf and a high rod doesn't hold much. Fortunately, any closet is a candidate for improvement.

Look for a modular system that makes it easy for kids to put stuff away. Closet stores and home centers stock adjustable components from poles to shelves to drawers and baskets. Many of these stores have designers available on staff to help you draw up a plan.

Install rods at kid-friendly heights and include pullout drawers or bins for folded clothes, a pile of shoes, or a collection of toys. Most important, select a system that can adapt to a growing child's changing needs.

Dressers and armoires

Along with a bed and a night table, a dresser will likely be one of the first pieces of furniture that you buy. If you choose a low dresser, say, with three drawers, a young child will be able to select his own clothes and put them away. Later you can add a matching unit to expand storage capacity. Highboy chests maximize storage when you are short on floor space, but they put most belongings out of reach of little kids. Custom storage units resolve unique storage challenges, but

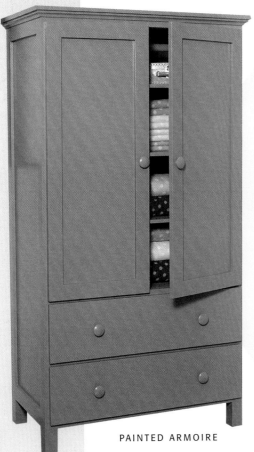

PAINTED ARMOIRE

CUBBY UNIT

keep in mind that built-in styles stay put if you move.

Armoires are freestanding closets. Most have a hanging rod, shelves, and drawers of sufficient capacity for a little one's possessions. Older kids will likely need additional storage, but a classic style will retain its usefulness—and appeal—throughout the teen years. Expect a teen to convert an armoire into an entertainment unit to hold a sound system, a television, games, CDs, and books.

Look for dressers, armoires, and chests that are sturdy and stable. Top-heavy units can tip over. For safety, secure tall chests to the wall with anchors or angle braces. Test the drawers: they should slide smoothly on glides and have stops to keep them from pulling out all the way.

Shelves, bookcases, cubbies

Furniture with shelves and cubbies or wall-hung systems with adjustable shelves will provide flexible storage for almost all a child's belongings. But a shelf's endless expanse invites disorder. Divide shelves into usable "drawers" with baskets and boxes. If your child is very messy, you might complement open storage with a set of cabinet doors to hide some of the chaos. As always, be sure to anchor a freestanding unit to the wall if it's at all wobbly.

MODULAR STORAGE PIECES

ADJUSTABLE CLOSET SYSTEM

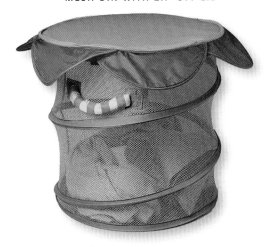

Underbed storage

To a parent, a messy jumble of toys, clothes, papers, and books is the real monster under a child's bed. Rolling underbed units (pictured on page 110) will tame the beast. They're available in many sizes through catalogs and stores that sell containers; measure the space below your child's bed to see what will fit.

A captain's bed already has built-in drawers below the mattress. Or opt for a trundle frame on casters and use it as one gigantic drawer (install dividers or you'll never be able to find anything).

Boxes, bins, baskets, tubs

Large drawers and toy chests are the black holes of kids' storage; toss blocks or crayons into either and you may never see them again. Tackle clutter instead with smaller containers, from wire buckets to flatware caddies to cardboard boxes—or even laundry baskets.

A wooden frame holding slide-out bins in vivid colors accommodates toys, stuffed animals, or sporting equipment. For easy retrieval, be sure that contents are visible or bins are labeled.

A container is not a one-size-fits-all solution. Choose one just big enough to hold a particular set or collection. Visit container and hardware stores for lots of ideas about how to match storage needs to containers.

WICKER BASKETS

For dirty clothes

Is the floor or the back of a chair your child's current hamper? Set a hamper near where kids undress so that it's a quick toss to stow dirty clothes. Almost any container of adequate size can serve as a hamper, from a basket to a simple bag on a frame to a mesh barrel with a top that unzips. Or play up the hoop dreams of a junior shooting guard with a hamper that's a basketball hoop and net.

Outside the box

Especially in a kid's room, just about any type of organizer or accessory can become a successful clutter buster. In fact, the more creative, the better. Unlikely storage aids not only help subdue the mess but also give a room personality.

Mount pegs or whimsical drawer pulls on the wall for hanging up tonight's pajamas and tomorrow's school clothes. Let kids stow socks, slippers, or doll collections in hanging or wall-mounted shoe bags, vinyl pouches, or net bags. Give stuffed animals or train sets a home in a canvas tote: it moves easily around the room, around the house, or to a play date. Stow a teen's CDs in a stack of spinning cubes or a nifty rack.

COLLAPSIBLE BOXES

FOLD-UP LAUNDRY
HAMPER

SLIDE-OUT PLASTIC
TUBS

STACKED
STORAGE CUBES

WOODEN PEGS

How to
DO IT

AS A KID, did you have a say in decorating your bedroom? If you loved the room you grew up in, chances are you were included in the planning. The most successful children's rooms—the ones that satisfy kids in every way (and that their parents can live with, too)—grow out of an ongoing collaboration between parent and child. Use this chapter to guide you through the steps that will marry kids' dreams with your practical realities.

Partners
in Planning

INVOLVING YOUR KIDS in the planning of their rooms has benefits that go beyond the final decor. They'll learn critical life skills, such as making choices and participating in discussions. And who knows? If kids truly love their rooms, maybe they'll even keep them neat! As step one, sit down together to go over the questions on the opposite page.

Let's face it. In a world filled with distractions from computers to cell phones, it can be tough to get your child's attention. But invite kids to help plan their room, and watch how fast they snap out of that video-game trance.

In an age-appropriate way, spell out the goal and the scope of the makeover based on the realities of budget, time, and givens like room size or available wall space. Think through the must-have elements of the room, from sleeping to storage. And let kids dream a little about what features would please them most.

Encourage them to express their likes and dislikes (prepare to be amazed at what you didn't know about your own kids). They might be shy at first, but you'll find them to be very definite about what they want. Write it all down (little kids can dictate their answers), completing the questionnaire on the next page or making up your own.

Understand their needs

Compare answers. You and the kids may be heading off in entirely different directions. Some probing on your part may be in order. Does your child really crave exactly the same bed as his friend Jake? Or is it just an iron headboard that he fancies, or the boldly striped blanket? Does he need blackout shades to sleep better, or to hide the scary tree outside his window? Is it a pink bed that she wants, or simply the color pink somewhere in the room? Is a big desk really necessary if the kitchen table is the favored spot for homework? The goal is to create an environment that is meaningful to the child who lives there. The more input you have from your kids, the more they will prize the result.

DREAM TEAM
Questionnaire

For Kids

1. Why do you want to change your room? _____

   What do you like about your room now? _____

   What don't you like? _____

2. What activities do you plan to do in the room? _____

   Where do you read? _____ Do you want a chair for reading or relaxing? ❑ Yes ❑ No

   Where do you study? _____ Do you use a computer? ❑ Yes ❑ No

3. What kind of bed do you like? _____ Do friends sleep over often? ❑ Yes ❑ No

4. How do you like to store your clothes? ❑ Folded ❑ Hung up ❑ Dropped in a basket

   Do you also need space to display collections and special stuff? ❑ Yes ❑ No

5. What are your favorite colors? _____

   How do you like your room? ❑ Bright and exciting ❑ Calm and quiet

6. Describe your perfect room. _____

For Parents

1. Why do you want to change the room? _____

   Which changes are "musts"? _____ Which are "dreams"? _____

2. What is working in the room now? _____

   What isn't working? _____

   What items will you keep? _____

   What will you need to purchase? _____

3. How long do you hope this new decor will last? _____

4. What is your budget? _____

5. How much time is available for the makeover? _____

   Will you do it all yourself? ❑ Yes ❑ No What outside help will you need? _____

6. Note any special challenges. ❑ Two kids sharing the room ❑ Allergies ❑ Not enough natural light

   ❑ Small closet ❑ Other _____

Before you start stripping wallpaper, swapping the bed, or pulling up the carpet, make a wish list with your child. The answers to the questions on this page will reveal dreams, help you set priorities, and pinpoint what goes where in the room. Make two copies of this questionnaire—one for you, one for your child. (If you need more space for answers, use another sheet of paper.) Before you begin filling in the blanks, you may want to take a look at the next two sections, "A Room Just for Me" and "Dreams versus Reality."

A Room
Just for Me

TO KIDS, the coolest bedrooms are the ones that truly reflect who they are. Hang a big bulletin board for posters of their favorite personalities of the moment, from sports heroes to rock stars. Create a tropical-themed retreat for a beach-loving teen. Give a soccer star plenty of shelf space for her trophies. Rescue kids' rooms from hotel blandness with an individual point of view—theirs!

Collections and displays

Kids love collecting stuff, including keepsakes of no apparent value to anyone but themselves. They're proud of their collections. They want to be able to look at them and show them off to friends and family. And as kids grow, they bring home memorabilia, awards, and trophies that demand display space alongside beloved toys and all manner of precious junk.

A bulletin board or display board of fabric or metal—the bigger the better—belongs in every kid's room. Beyond treasures that can hang from pushpins or magnets, let the collection dictate how you will display it. Shelves, whether they're part of a bookcase or fixed to the wall, suit everything from dolls to stuffed animals to rocks. Install a cantilevered shelf over a door or at picture-rail height (about 72 inches from the floor) for

Left: A budding astronaut chose wallpaper with vintage spaceships to complement a collection of model rockets. The room can easily be redone should the child switch career paths.

collections that stay put. A shelf above a window can do dual duty, serving as a valance as well as storage.

Get creative. Show off a rotating display of your child's latest masterpieces with a simple system of clips attached to a board or clothesline. Arrange a hat collection on pegs that run the length of the wall, a purse collection on an antique coat rack. Suspend model planes from the ceiling. Attach whimsical birdhouses to a faux tree painted on the wall. Fill a shadowbox with fossils, miniature cars, or snow globes.

Theme rooms

If your child fancies living in the cockpit of an airplane, under the sea, or out on the prairie, decorating the room is easy. A theme is a visual narrative that guides choices from bedding to wall coverings to accessories. Assembling the components is fun for both of you.

On the other hand, this year's pilot may be next year's paleontologist. Out goes the airplane light fixture; in come the dinosaur sheets. Kids'

Top right: A bulletin board holds pride of place above an expansive desk, allowing a curious child to show off a current passion—bugs today, something new tomorrow.

Bottom right: This room gets its rah-rah spirit from spreads made of vintage wool felt pennants. Red-framed wooden beds with star cutouts support the pennants' vibrant colors, all set off by soft yellow walls.

interests are apt to change rapidly. You save work and money if you restrict expression of the theme to items that are easily swapped—a comforter, curtains, or a wallpaper border, for instance. A more lasting theme is one that reflects a child's long-standing interest—like music, astronomy, competitive sports, or horseback riding—or a family interest such as sailing or the outdoors.

Boy rooms/girl rooms

Do girls still like pink beds and flowers on their sheets? Do boys still sleep in rooms that look as if they've been furnished by a college athletic department? These aren't sets from a 1950s movie. These stereotypes live on in many kids' rooms. Just browse the catalogs or the aisles of furniture stores. Well, *vive la différence!* In a world where gender barriers are falling, many kids still choose colors, patterns, and themes right out of "Leave It to Beaver." Simply enjoy it. Choices abound in appealing bedding and accessories for tradition-minded kids, updated by designers with fresh hues and patterns.

They love it/you hate it

She wants purple walls. He wants to sleep in a bed that looks like a Porsche. If you've told your

kids "anything goes" in their room, can you live with (or afford) the result? A better way is to ask their opinions and be willing to compromise. If total vivid purple is out of the question, offer to paint her closet purple or use purple throw pillows and matching area rug. Be frank if a custom car bed is too expensive, but suggest a gallery trip to select automobile posters for his walls.

Rescue kids' rooms from hotel blandness with an individual point of view—theirs!

Preselecting choices is another win-win scenario. Do some homework before offering your child options. Then say, "We're getting this bed. Is your favorite green or blue?" Don't hesitate to present kids with a number of choices. You'll find them quick to make decisions about what they like.

Outside help in the form of a neutral third party—a professional designer or a knowledgeable sales associate—can mediate a standoff between parent and child, especially with older kids. Design services for everything from creating floor plans to suggesting products to coordinating paint, fabric, and color selections are available at many home centers and furniture retailers.

Facing page: Mom might have grown up with pink walls and a classic iron bed, too. But an energized color scheme and lively bedding give the daughter's room a look that's fresh and new.

PICTURING
My Dream Room

"Go to your room!" If they love their bedrooms, will kids misbehave just to invoke that classic parental banishment? We hope not. But if their rooms are as unique as the kids themselves, they become more than just places to sleep, dress, and do homework. They also serve as child-friendly havens in a world designed by, and for, grown-ups.

So what do kids want? Pink flowers, a stage for a preteen star, room for books, no room for a pesky sister. Let your child's wish list start the room-planning process (see "Dream Team Questionnaire," page 91). Some ideas may be workable just as they are, while others may need a little refinement. Even the most way-out fantasies may spark more practical inspirations.

Each of the five rooms pictured on these two pages would be a dream come true for the real kid who designed it.

Kelly, age 12: "My room would be a place where I can relax and do whatever I want. When I'm in my room I can forget about all my problems. I can listen to music and dance freely."

Emma, age 10: "Green, blue, and gray are must-have colors in my room. I also definitely need a computer, a lot of books, and tons of cats."

Maddie, age 9: "My dream room has a big screen TV so I can watch DVDs and videos. It has two beds, one for me and one is for my best friend, she lives with me. We picked the colors pink and yellow because my best friend's favorite color is pink and my favorite color is yellow."

Kevin, age 10: "This picture is about my dream room. I like this room because I have my bed and my Xbox, and my dog."

Nicholas, age 8: "My bedroom is neat! I can do all sorts of bedroom stuff like computer games, make Lego robots, read books, and hide things in a secret door. My secret door is behind my shelf and I can go in it. When I look out my window, I can see my beautiful back yard. Best of all there is no bed for my sister."

Dreams
versus Reality

YOU'VE MADE A WISH LIST that captures the room as it is now and as you and your child hope to improve it. But how often do we discover that what we dream of and what is actually possible are at odds? It's time to review the questionnaire on page 91 and make some basic decisions. Your answers will help you develop a plan that's right for you, your child, and the room.

What must the room do?

Kids really *live* in their rooms. Decide exactly what activities will take place there besides sleeping—playing, studying, reading, listening to music, entertaining friends. Define an area for each, then figure out how to make it work. The result will be a pleasing, personal space that truly reflects—and delights—its occupant.

Sleeping. The sleeping area is the most important part of the room. Start with the obvious: don't block doors, windows, or heating vents. Avoid putting the bed under a window if the child is very young and could possibly climb out, or if you live in an earthquake-prone region where temblors might rattle or even break window glass. A more secure location is a corner where walls will protect the bed on two sides.

Left: "Spin art" inspired this glossy table and chairs that the Jetson kids of cartoon fame would certainly covet. The tabletop actually spins. While it looks retro, the set is new, as is the tweedy shag rug, its style soul mate.

Playtime. Open floor space is critical for play, especially in a young child's room. Kids of all ages like to sprawl on the floor with games or a book. Some playthings require a smooth, level surface, while others work fine on carpeting. A hard surface through most of the room, with throw rugs for comfort, handles all types of play. For quiet play, kids love nooks and hideaways such as a cozy window seat or even a bed draped like a tent.

Study. A well-designed study area includes a work surface (at least 2 feet deep and 4 feet wide), a comfortable chair, and good lighting. Computer equipment requires extra space. Nearby bookshelves and drawers keep supplies within easy reach and encourage neatness and organization. Some kids are easily distracted if the study area is in front of a window or if the desk chair can swivel. Plan accordingly.

Storage. Grown-ups want to hide belongings that aren't in constant use, but kids don't. The idea is to organize the clutter so that the room looks neat yet the child knows where to find things. Keep articles in sight, arranged on open shelves or stashed

Top right: Outfitted with a floating shelf, a corner becomes an area for study and art projects. The colorful chairs are both stable and easy for kids to move around.

Bottom right: An intimate sleeping area like this one is especially hospitable to younger kids, who prefer cozy spaces.

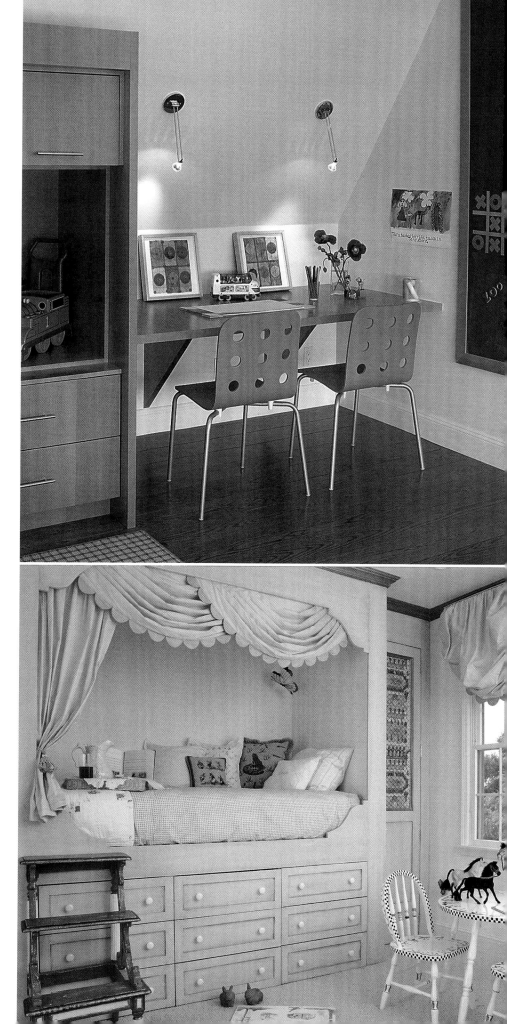

in boxes, bins, or other containers. Fix pegs or rods at kid-friendly height to hang clothes, supplemented by drawers for items that are stored folded.

Identify the givens

Your child's wish list may be long, but a good life exercise is to filter his or her dreams (and yours) through a screen of reality. What elements *must* stay? What objects do you want to keep because they're truly loved (an heirloom chest, for example)? What *must* be changed? What already works in the room? What are the challenges?

The physical layout. Not only the room dimensions but also the locations of windows, doors, electrical outlets, telephone jacks, and heating vents dictate many decorating decisions. So do architectural flaws such as low ceilings, limited wall space, awkward ceilings, or lack of natural light. Light and bright colors, creative furniture placement, and clever use of paint can camouflage problems.

Location. The room's location has great impact, too. The sound of incessant music or boisterous play from kids' quarters may rocket noise control to the top of your list of priorities. In that case, you'll want to choose materials that will deaden sound: wall-to-wall carpeting, cork flooring, a large area rug, or sound-

Is it a wall or the ceiling? This room's decor skirts the issue with paint, transforming an awkward slope into a backdrop for a built-in captain's bed (partly seen at right).

absorbing accessories like huge cork bulletin boards.

Maintenance. Real kids live in your house. They create messes. Make it easy for you and for them by furnishing their rooms with durable materials that resist stains and dirt. The younger or more careless the child, the tougher and easier to clean the room surfaces should be. Look for hard-wearing, spillproof, dirt-resistant treatments for the floor, walls, and furnishings. Good choices include scrubbable vinyl wallpaper, wood with a waterproof finish, and laminate tabletops. Choose washable fabrics.

Resources and budget. Budget is a critical consideration. Be open with your kids about what's financially feasible. Pinpoint the "musts" on your list, then try to include as many of their dreams as you can. Calculate the time, energy, and skills—yours or those of professional designers, contractors, and installers—that will be available to complete the project. Plan for success: a realistic assessment of what is possible all around will head off disappointment, headaches, and delays later on.

Sharing a room. A kid's dream room probably doesn't include a sibling in the next bed. But in the real world, brothers or sisters often live in close quarters. Make the best of togetherness by designing a room that is personal for each child.

Two beds (or more) are a given. But kids who share a room need to claim ownership of other territory, too. A desk of one's own is prime real estate for any child, but especially one living with a sibling. Assign kids their own drawers and closet space as well, and provide each with a place for hobby gear and displays. Unless both roommates fancy the same theme, let them express their individuality. Get personal with the same bedding in two different colors. Accent each bed with monogrammed cushions. Put a small chest of slightly different design at the foot of each bed. Give each child a bulletin board.

Above: A room that sizzles was the request. Heavy-duty enamel in brilliant tangerine-orange and neon pink gives a glossy shine, a hard finish, and a fun look to plain furniture. On the floor are inexpensive, hardworking linoleum squares in eye-popping colors. The butterfly chair (top photo) first saw duty in a grandparents' apartment fifty years ago. It was revived with a new powder-coat finish in blazing orange.

Ages
and Stages

IS THAT MY KID? Children change so quickly that it can seem as if an entirely new person has moved in. Be aware that kids' rooms need to mirror and support each stage of their development. Here we summarize some basic requirements for different age groups. Use these as guidelines to help you adapt your child's space to his or her current needs and desires.

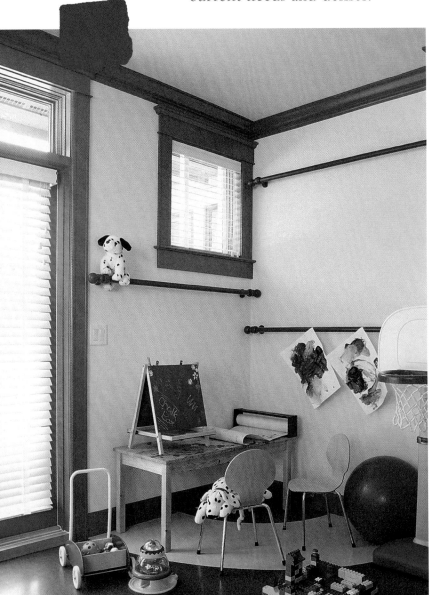

Three to five: room for exploration

Have pith helmet ready when you design a room for your preschooler, the in-house explorer. Fueled by a boundless curiosity and an active imagination, kids this age climb on everything, take things apart, and poke into everything they can reach. Keeping safety in mind, stock the room with sturdy, tip-proof furnishings and store breakables out of reach. Walls should be washable, floors hard-wearing and easy to clean.

Basic furnishings include a standard-size bed (with or without removable rails), a nightstand, and a bedside light. A dresser, stackable drawers, or a wardrobe with plenty of shelf space will likely handle clothing storage for now. For play, include an area for drawing, working puzzles, and building things—favorite preschool activities that foster reading and writing skills.

Left: Perfect in every way for a preschooler, this room has bright colors, durable surfaces that are easy to care for, and pint-size furnishings.

Preschool children are extroverts who respond to bright, energetic hues, balanced by softer, soothing tones. They love color in their rooms. Color-coded storage—blue for toys, green for clothes, for example—encourages cleanup and teaches association. A simple storage system that's easy to figure out also helps kids develop a sense of order. Provide low shelves so that possessions are accessible and easy to put away, and use small bins (large bins create a confusing mess when contents are dumped out).

Six to eight: growing up

When kids gear up for school, so must their bedrooms. It's time to replace (or supplement) child-size table and chairs with a desk of some sort, even if schoolwork is regularly done at the kitchen table. Kids love a desk because they can control what's on it, in a "hands off, it's mine" sort of way that's very meaningful to them. Add task lighting for homework and reading areas. Provide several seating options—a formal chair for the desk, a more

Top right: Available in many styles, a trundle bed is a space-saving solution for sleepovers. It's a particularly sensible alternative to bunk beds for younger kids who may still be fearful of heights.

Bottom right: Thanks to bunk beds, most of the floor space in this grade-schooler's room is available for hanging out. The lower bunk is an adult-size double bed that will hold its appeal through the teen years.

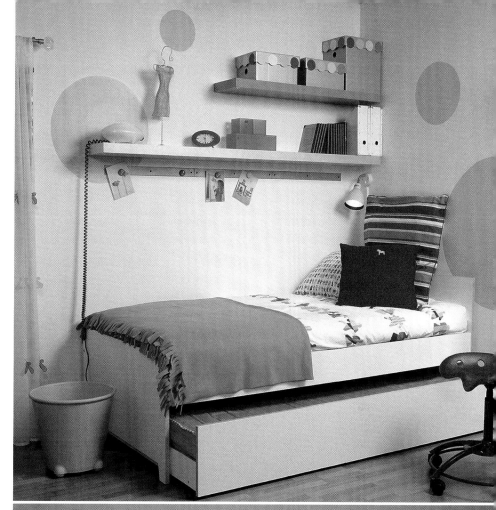

casual, comfy spot for lounging. Kids also like to flop on their bed, sink into a beanbag chair, sprawl on a cushy floor pillow, or stretch out on a rug.

Requests for sleepovers start, prompted by an expanding social life. Get set for overnight guests with a bunk bed, a trundle bed, a chair that converts to a bed, or slip-covered foam slabs that store under a standard bed.

Well-organized storage will control the clutter of school supplies, toys, and clothes. Dedicate storage areas for specific uses—toys here, homework there. Add more shelf space if you can.

Kids' rooms need to mirror and support each stage of their development.

Nine to twelve: transition

Get ready. They've definitely crossed a line. Recognize preteens by their sprouting collections, sports and hobby equipment, precious junk, and strong sense of what (they think) they want. More say in room decor is at the top of the list. The basic elements of their bedroom—adult-size bed, dresser, and night table—remain the same. But banished is anything they view as remotely babyish. Updated bedding, fresh colors, and fun accessories set a scene to a preteen's liking.

Factor technology into any room plan: your child will be ready for a computer in the room unless the family shares one elsewhere in the house. Find a spot for preteen fixtures such as a sound system or electronic games and accessories.

Possessions multiply. Scrutinize every surface for storage potential—on walls and in corners, above doors, below windows, under beds, on shelves, in baskets, inside cabinets. Head off holes in the wall, chipped paint, and arguments: install a permanent display board (as large as possible) for rotating collections of the latest posters, postcards, and photos.

Teens: declaration of independence

You call it their bedroom. But "studio apartment" better describes the way teenagers view their personal space. Privacy is a paramount desire. You don't cross a threshold when you enter the bedroom of a teenager, you cross a border. Teens feel that theirs is a private domain, to be run without interference.

More than ever, teenagers want a place to sleep, a place to study, and cushy seating for hanging out with friends. "My way" is how they want it furnished. The challenge: to let your teen reinvent the room in a way both of you can live with. Create a budget, specify what can be changed, promise an open mind, but retain final veto power; it's your house, after all. Then turn the project over to the teens, a vote of confidence they'll prize.

More grown-up furnishings—if there's room—might range from a larger bed to a sofa-like daybed or a small couch. Expect a new color scheme, perhaps based on a sports team, current fashion, or a lifelong passion for a particular hue. Be sure your teenager has good study space with plenty of room to sprawl. Encourage (but don't expect) neatness with well-organized storage space.

Left: Placing the bed in an alcove made this sunny room appear larger. Hot colors, a fanciful wood valance, and a "headboard" painted on the wall create a theatrical backdrop that just about any preteen girl would love.

Below: This teen's "X-treme" room is bursting with surf, ski, and skateboard images. A cork valance over the blinds serves as a keepsake bulletin board.

Rooms
That Last

DESIGNERS SAY that a good decorating scheme will continue to look fresh for five to seven years. Even then, you won't have to completely refurbish the room if the plan is flexible. Buy adaptable furniture that can grow with the child. Then update the decor with age-appropriate accessories—framed pages from children's books for a preschooler, movie posters later on.

Good news! Kids' furniture is the new darling of the home furnishings world. Manufacturers have drafted the best design talent to develop their children's collections—and it shows. You'll find multipiece groupings for toddlers to teens, designed with color, whimsy, durability, and lots of style.

Good for the long haul, functional furnishings purchased as separate modules can grow with your child by recombining to suit changing needs. Components may include beds, drawers, cabinets, shelving, work surfaces, and storage units. Also investigate the bounty available at home storage centers, including sturdy stacking drawers and stacking bins. Start low and then stack higher as your child gains inches.

Kids, especially little ones, thrive in an environment that "fits" them. Practical

Left: Orange walls and furnishings in sage green and yellow give this room a playful sophistication suitable for kids of all ages. A cozy chair is the perfect retreat for reading.

options that deliver years of use include beds that can be raised or lowered, beds that can be extended from junior to adult length, and office-style chairs with adjustable seats, backs, and arms. Bunk beds that unstack into twin beds accommodate the ups and downs of kids' changing sleeping habits.

Buy adaptable furniture that can grow with the child, and update it with accessories.

Hand-me-down treasures not only add warmth, they also connect generations and speak of family traditions. A vintage chest, a retro bedside table, or your own childhood chair has a mellow patina that kids respond to in a room otherwise filled with bright, new pieces.

Top right: Family heirlooms add atmosphere and a sense of history to kids' rooms. This whitewashed pedestal table has been passed down through four generations of one family.

Bottom right: This sleigh bed once belonged to the mother of the girl who sleeps in it now, as did the dollhouse.

DESIGNED
with Room to Grow

Good thing kids don't outgrow their rooms as often as they do their clothes. Start with a flexible plan, and you can design a room that fits your child from preschool to high school with only minor alterations. The key is choosing core furnishings that meet kids' long-term needs, updated over the years with fresh accessories and accent pieces. The child that moves into this room at age 3 will find the space just as pleasing at age 15.

Ages 3 to 5 ▶

Light wood furnishings set off the bright primary colors that preschoolers love. The basics are a platform bed with storage beneath and in the headboard, a three-drawer dresser, and a four-niche cubby on a one-drawer base. Accent pieces: two bookcases, a storage bench, two bins, and a kid-size table and chairs. Walls: wallpaper with a border at kid's-eye height. Window: a light-blocking shade and simple fabric panels. Floor: hardwood with multicolor area rug.

Ages 6 to 8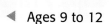

A revised floor plan creates areas for doing school-work and lounging with friends. New: a desk with hutch, a desk chair, two beanbag chairs, wallpaper and border, and a display board. Passed along to a younger sibling: the storage bench, the bins, and the table and chairs.

Ages 9 to 12

For a child who's growing up, storage pieces are reconfigured. New: a twin-over-full bunk bed (great for sleepovers), an armoire, a mobile night table, a second cubby and base, vibrant bedding, a more grown-up area rug, and wallpaper and border. Passed along: the platform bed and the multicolor area rug.

Teens ▶

Welcome to the studio apartment. The armoire is now an entertainment unit, and the bed is the double from the bunk bed set. New: a high chest, a modern desk, a metal-and-glass display cabinet, bedding, painted walls, and wooden window blinds. Passed along: the twin bunk bed, the blue bookcases, the student desk and hutch, two low base units, and one cubby.

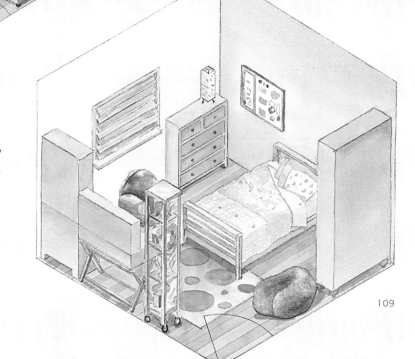

109

Storage
Clean and Simple

SOME KIDS THRIVE IN CLUTTER, but most don't really function well in a messy room or one that's packed with an over-abundance of possessions. The key to a neat and functional space is to organize belongings with effective, age-appropriate storage. When everything has a home, kids can find what they need easily and then stow it away just as easily later on.

Divide and conquer

Good storage encourages more than just cleanup. It helps kids track their possessions, develop a sense of order, become self-sufficient, and focus their attention. Young children in particular like to see what they have. They want to display their stuff, not hide it behind closed doors. Furniture with shelves, compartments, or cubbies will hold baskets, buckets, or bins to corral the clutter, letting kids stash their stuff but still keep it all in plain sight. For preschoolers, use low shelves for the toys they use every day, higher ones for the stuff that's used less often.

Assign everything a home, and containerize as much as possible. Contents should be clearly visible. If they're not, offer a visual clue of what's inside, such as a photo or an icon drawn by the child. Or code with color—red for shoes, green for toys, blue for puzzles.

Left: Rolling bins that slide under the bed organize a potentially terrifying quantity of toys. Open storage like this keeps everything in sight, with toys kids use most often readily accessible.

Match the size of the container to the objects it holds—a bucket just the right size for a set of blocks, for example, or a bag for all the crayons. That lets kids remove and return just what they want without pulling out everything they own.

Young children do best with small containers, which hold less and are easier to tote around; older children can sort through larger ones. If containers are too large, though, your child (and you) might forget what's inside. Besides, a giant bin takes up too much play space.

Less is more

A successful storage system calls for regular editing. Have on hand just what excites your child at that moment. Young kids especially may want it all, but in reality they can't handle as many choices as their older siblings, experts say. Subdue chaos by paring down what's out at any one time. Rotate prized possessions to keep interest high; in consultation with your child, give away those that are out of favor. What about clothing? Kids, especially teens, seem to sprout inches from one week to the next. Does it still fit? Do they still wear it? If not, move it out of the room—for the season or permanently.

Top right: The pockets of a hanging shoe bag both display and store a doll collection.

Bottom right: Wall-mounted racks keep favorite picture books within easy reach.

If storage is limited, dedicate a closet or cabinet elsewhere in the house to family games, arranged so your kids can reach them. Treasured objects like stuffed animals or old trophies that are too dear to hide away are best displayed in sight but out of the way. A shelf above a door or window or a high one that runs around the whole room is perfect for such collections.

Give them options

Engage your child's interest and make cleanup fun by combining traditional bookcases, armoires, cubbies, and shelves with more creative storage solutions. Be inventive: stored objects needn't line up like cars in a garage, they just need to be contained. Toss sports shoes in one crate, sports equipment in another. Store a train set in a canvas tote, handy to move around the house.

Fixed options include peg-shelf combinations or single pegs, hooks, and knobs. Hanging pockets and shoe bags made of fabric or clear vinyl are useful for organizing small items, from action figures to markers and crayons to an expanding handbag collection—and they're easy to raise as your child grows. Portable containers include all sorts of pails, totes, baskets, bins on wheels, hatboxes, and stacking crates.

Take inspiration from schools and libraries, experts at durable, convenient, kid-friendly storage. Use wall-mounted racks to keep books and schoolwork at hand, or drape current magazines over rods fixed to the wall. For a look at other storage solutions, turn to pages 84–87.

Closets

Position hooks and rods low to encourage little kids to hang up their clothes. However, most young kids don't have much to hang up. One or two low rods in the closet may be all they need. If you install one rod above the other, you can reserve the upper rod for out-of-season storage. Outfit the rest of the closet with drawers and shelves. The most practical solution is a closet system

that can be reconfigured as the child (and the wardrobe) grows.

Space-saving storage

Make small rooms seem larger with efficient storage that frees up floor space. Hang hooks, shoe bags, and pouches on chair-rail molding or on door backs. Take advantage of the fact that kids love to stash stuff under their beds: look for drawers or shallow bins on wheels that fit beneath the bed. Incorporate multi-purpose pieces—a headboard or bench with storage inside, or a desk-hutch combination that includes a bookshelf and perhaps built-in lighting.

Some kids prefer to store clothes folded; think about removing the closet door entirely and filling the niche with a dresser, chest, or shelves.

Top right: A hanging book rack could easily serve as bedside storage in a small room.

Bottom right: Divide kids' closets into compartments that offer storage options: shelves, bins, and rods.

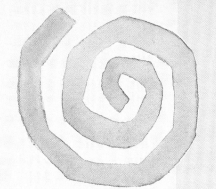

DEALING
with Allergies

Many materials and finishes can irritate kids who have chemical sensitivities. In addition, household dust harbors allergy-provoking dust mites. Minimizing allergens in a child's room involves careful selection of its contents as well as frequent cleaning. Keep the room neat and surfaces uncluttered so they can be dusted or vacuumed two or three times a week. Use nontoxic cleaning products.

Carpet. Avoid wall-to-wall carpeting if your child is allergic. Besides harboring dust mites, mold, pesticides tracked in on shoes, and other allergens, carpet often is treated with products that trigger sensitivities. If carpet can't be avoided, choose one with low pile and no permanent or moth-repellent chemicals, and consider banning shoes from the room or wearing indoor-only shoes.

Ask your installer to air out the carpet off-site and install it with tack strips and adhesive tape. If adhesive is unavoidable, use low-emitting, solvent-free adhesives to reduce installation emissions. Ventilate the room well during installation and for at least several weeks afterward. Clean the carpet frequently with a HEPA vacuum cleaner. Throw rugs are okay to use if they can be washed.

Smooth-surface floors. Glazed ceramic tile, linoleum, and hardwood are good flooring choices—they don't collect dust and are easy to clean. Use a no-VOC (volatile organic compounds), water-based finish on hardwood floors; it will emit fewer toxic fumes than an oil-based one. Ask your floor installer to use only nails, not

adhesive; if adhesive is unavoidable, ask for the low-emitting, solvent-free type. Ventilate the room well during installation and for at least several weeks afterward.

Paint. Oil-based paints emit high levels of toxic fumes that may be inhaled even after application and drying, as the paint cures. In kids' rooms, experts suggest instead using no-VOC, water-based latex paint that contains fewer solvents and gives off less odor. Keep the room well ventilated even after the odor disappears.

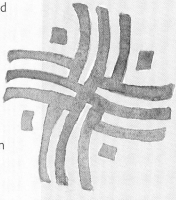

Bedding. Cut down on exposure to dust mites by encasing mattress, box spring, pillows, and comforter in dust-mite barrier covers, tightly woven synthetic protectors that zip shut. Use hypoallergenic pillows rather than down or feathers, which get dusty and attract dust mites. Be sure to wash sheets, pillowcases, and comforter covers frequently in hot water—at least 130°F—in order to to kill mites.

Furniture. Solid-wood pieces with no-VOC, water-based finishes work best for most kids who have chemical sensitivities. Upholstered furniture collects dust; consider wood-framed pieces with washable cushions and covers instead. Toys and books that sit on a shelf are also dust catchers. For children with severe allergies, minimize dust by storing toys in a closed chest and books behind see-through doors.

Walls, Floors, *and Windows*

KIDS ARE AWARE of every surface in their rooms. The floor is both territory to walk across and a place to lounge. Walls set the scene as well as provide shelter. Windows connect kids with the outdoors and supply natural lighting. In order to make the most of each surface, take time to think about which materials and finishes will best suit your child's room.

Walls and ceilings

Children are comforted, not confined, by walls and ceilings—so much so that they want to personalize every square foot with fun colors and patterns. Expect the unexpected in a world created by and for a kid: a purple closet, polka-dot walls, gold stars spilling across an indigo ceiling. A little paint or wallpaper will work magic; for some shopping guidelines, see pages 64–65. But where does one begin?

Paint. Nothing freshens and lifts a room like paint. Start by selecting the color. You can keep it simple—a solid color on the walls and ceiling, with a contrasting trim. Or you can add visual punch with an accent color, perhaps on the wall behind the bed or around a window. Use blackboard paint behind the desk. Or let the walls be neutral and showcase the ceiling (a main focus of your child's

Left: Coordinating patterns create a serene scheme in lavender and white. Wallpaper gives plain walls architectural interest—creating a wainscot and also accenting a window.

reflective time): cover it with dreamy floating clouds or a school of deep-sea creatures.

Give walls and ceilings star quality with decorative paint treatments. Add whimsy with simple stenciled motifs arranged as a border, scattered around a window, or encircling a light fixture. Kids adept with rubber stamps might enjoy stamping patterns on their walls (use a color that complements the base coat yet stands out from it).

For details on various special painting techniques, see the Sunset book *Faux and Decorative Painting* or consult the experts at your local paint store or home improvement center. Or you can hire a professional—a good plan if the design is an elaborate mural. Keep in mind, though, that wall murals are expensive and can be limiting. One alternative is a scene painted on canvas and secured to the wall with hooks and picture wire, letting you change decor almost as quickly as kids change their interests.

Wallpaper. A favorite designer's tool to hide imperfect walls, wallpaper can visually raise a low ceiling, decorate at a kid's eye level, or give a room instant personality. For wallpaper

with staying power, avoid trendy patterns and cartoon characters. Also consider upkeep; wallpapers that are washable and stain resistant rate high with parents of young kids. If the room gets lots of sunlight, ask to see colorfast wallpapers; if the room is small enough that bumping against the walls is inevitable, consider abrasion-resistant ones.

Coordinating borders are an attractive finish for wallpaper or an easy

accent on a painted wall—and they can be installed in less than an hour. You can apply a border at virtually any height, from the point where the wall meets the ceiling on down. Let a border frame a window, create a chair rail, separate two paint colors, or enhance a baseboard.

Flooring

For little ones, the floor is a construction zone. Older kids claim it as their personal lounge for reading, listening to music, playing games, and hanging out with friends. Look for comfort, ease of care, and durability when selecting flooring. For active play, choose a smooth surface like wood or a resilient material such as vinyl or linoleum. For warmth and softness as well as sound control, use carpeting or an area rug. For a discussion of flooring choices, see pages 52–55.

A combination of floor surfaces works well. A shaggy throw rug over a sleek linoleum or wood floor does dual duty; the rug is a cozy oasis that anchors a bed or chair and defines an area for activities, while the smooth surface is a flat, low-maintenance area for racing cars or stacking blocks. The reverse works, too: layer a "rug" of resilient flooring over wall-to-wall carpeting, as shown in the photo at top right.

A painted floorcloth is a fun alternative to conventional carpeting that can be rolled up for storage. It protects the permanent floor surface, too. Hire an artist or paint it yourself on primed floorcloth canvas, available at art supply stores, and protect the design with a clear sealer.

Top right: An artistic nine-year-old selected bright red and green as trim for his room. The playful bull's-eye "rug" was custom-made of concentric rings of linoleum.

Bottom right: Rather than downplay the deep dormer window, this room's occupant chose to set off both window and view with wallpaper and tieback curtains.

SEEING
the Light

Good lighting extends daylight and defines activity areas in a child's room. A well-lit room incorporates several types of lighting.

Ambient light, usually from a ceiling fixture, provides soft, general illumination. Since kids are most comfortable entering a room that's already lit, have a switch near the door to turn on at least one light, if possible. Stronger, more focused task light supplements ambient light, defining areas for reading or attacking homework.

Simple or elaborate night-lights or strings of whimsical novelty lights cast a soft glow that cuts the darkness for kids who need it. Use decorative accent light to highlight a special collection. Pen-

dant fixtures hung over activity areas cast warm pools of light and "lower" a high ceiling.

For overall illumination for very young kids, out-of-reach ceiling fixtures are safest. For older kids, plan on a bedside light, either a table lamp, a clip-on light secured to the headboard, or a swing-arm lamp attached to the wall. As kids grow, add task lighting for projects and puzzles, and later for schoolwork. A dimmer increases lighting options.

Keep young eyes fresh by using task and general lighting together. Task light by itself creates glare and shadows, strong contrasts that strain eyes. Fix task lighting at the proper height for kids; it should light the work area, but the bulb should be blocked from view when they're seated next to the fixture. Overhead light is best for computer work; light from the side or behind the screen will create glare.

For a look at a variety of lighting fixtures for kids' rooms, turn to pages 66–67.

Window treatments

Through a window, children can chronicle seasons and weather, the life of a garden, the night sky, local birds, visiting creatures—the outside world as observed from the safe haven of their room. Children thrive in natural light, learning about time from its subtle, changing cues.

A well-chosen window treatment plays many roles in a child's room. Letting the light in is the primary function, but a window covering also blocks light for sleeping and provides privacy. It enhances decor and can visually correct architectural flaws

like small or oddly placed windows. For a discussion of various window coverings, turn to page 50. If privacy isn't an issue, your child may be happiest with uncovered windows.

Does your child require a dark room for sleeping? If so, incorporate light-blocking shades, blinds, or shutters (add softness with a valance or curtains, if desired). Does the window face the street, or the house next door? Adjustable blinds admit light but offer privacy. Is the room very sunny? Sheer curtains will filter light but not block it entirely. Is the view worth enhancing? Choose an

unobtrusive window treatment. Downplay an unattractive view with bold patterns and colors, or obscure it with sheer or semisheer fabrics.

Be sure the controls for window coverings are ones your child can operate safely. Keep drapery, shade, and blind cords out of reach of young children. If you don't want to cut a long cord, wrap it around a cleat mounted high on the wall. Or ask about the availability of a cordless lift system or shortened cords and wands when you purchase your window covering.

Putting It
All Together

IT'S TIME for all the design details to come together. But before you go shopping, you need to know how much furniture your room can hold and what the best furniture arrangement will be. To figure that out you need an accurate picture of the existing space—a floor plan. At the same time, you want to select the room colors, the most exciting decision for most kids.

Planning on paper

A floor plan that depicts actual space is a useful reality check. It allows you to try out multiple designs before you make a purchase or commit to a specific decor. And if you're short on ideas, the process of mapping out the room may inspire you.

It's helpful to start by making a rough sketch of the room, including the locations of electrical outlets, light switches, permanent light fixtures, telephone jacks, and heating vents. You'll use this sketch for recording accurate measurements, the next step. Be sure to mark the locations of doors and windows, and draw arcs to indicate which way the doors and any casement windows swing. Note window dimensions, including height above the floor, and all architectural trim that might affect furniture placement, window treatments, or wall-covering calculations.

Left: In this beautifully planned room, a playful fabric pattern of alphabet letters in warm and sunny hues inspired the rest of the decor.

Measure the room. Jot down each measurement on your rough sketch as you work your way around the room. Don't forget the closet; in small rooms, the closet is valuable space that might hold a freestanding storage piece or even a desk.

Using the measurements you've recorded, now draw the room to exact scale on graph paper. You can also use an acetate grid sheet and movable furniture templates, available at art supply stores. Or create floor plans and elevations easily and quickly with a computer and home design software program.

Develop your ideas. Now that you have drawn an accurate floor plan, use it to play around with furniture placement. Try out different arrangements using furniture templates on photocopies of the floor plan, layer tracing paper over the graph paper, or work on a computer. You can purchase ready-made templates at art supply stores or make your own paper cutouts of the furniture pieces you've selected.

Top right: Casual seating was a priority in this teen's room. Armless upholstered chairs and floor pillows offer plenty of options for lounging.

Bottom right: This cheerful room succeeds thanks to an analogous color scheme, combining hues that lie side by side on the color wheel. Use the colors in different amounts to avoid monotony, and add one contrasting accent.

Unless you plan to change the locations of outlets, switches, jacks, or vents, keep them in mind as you place the furniture. Be sure to leave enough room to open doors fully, pull back chairs, extend drawers, and make the bed.

Draw elevations. Test your favorite furniture arrangements by viewing them in elevation, as illustrated on pages 122–123. Like snapshots of the finished room, elevation drawings show furnishings and key accessories against the walls.

Follow the same steps as you did for the floor plan: transfer your basic measurements for each wall to graph paper or the computer. Make a copy for each furniture arrangement you want to try, or work on tracing paper overlays. Draw in the furniture, to scale, and add a color scheme with pencils, crayons, or marking pens.

Below: An antique armoire reflects a papier-mâché rocking rabbit.

Color their world

We color our world as we see it. Kids often paint theirs in wild combinations. Color is the first thing cited by children, especially young ones, to describe their dream room. A favorite color is an easy starting point for a kid's room—whether it's chosen from a paint chip, suggested by a cherished toy, inspired by the pattern of a comforter, or excerpted from the bold graphics of a poster.

Offer options, test them out. You want your kids to be surrounded with the colors they love, but how can you steer them to hues that you can live with, too? The scheme also needs to be one they won't tire of quickly. It's easy to change the color of a throw rug, not so easy to redo a whole room.

Be thrilled if your child's initial color selections please you both. Otherwise, compromise all around is the key. Arm your kids with color options inspired by their dream hues but edited by you—pumpkin and khaki, perhaps, instead of Popsicle orange and Goth black. Give them ideas on how to use the colors, and enjoy the fun as they get caught up in the project.

Remember that colors don't exist in isolation. Types of light, varying textures, and adjacent hues transform color in amazing ways. Audition the palette in your child's room for a few days. See how it looks in changing daylight and at night when you switch on a lamp. Study how colors and patterns work together. If you can, paint color swatches on the walls, preferably on two different planes— both walls of a corner, for example. Ask if your paint store sells super-size color chips that you can tape to the wall. Or paint color on a large piece of foam core board and move it around the room. You'll soon know if it's right for your kids, for you, and for the room.

Anything goes—somewhere. Later on, your kids may thank you for not drenching their room in surfer teal or princess pink. But right now, they're finding it hard to be gracious. Acknowledge their developing tastes: work in a version of their favorite color somewhere in the room, even if you hate it.

Blackboard paint is a win-win solution if your child requests black in the color scheme. Use it to transform a closet door, wainscoting, or the space between a desktop and a hanging bookshelf into a practical surface for scribbling. And it's easy to re-cover a pile of pillows, replace a throw, or repaint the inside of the closet later on with the next must-have hue. Who knows—you might even end up liking it.

Facing page: A color scheme of ocean blue and cloud white seems just right for a kid with a passion for sailing. The display of trophies and hats spanning an overhead beam makes clever use of an out-of-the-way architectural feature.

PICTURING
Your Room Plan

If you were designing a room for a nine-year-old girl—a soccer star—who likes drums and the color pink, needs room for sleepovers and lots of storage, and wants display space for trophies and a cozy reading nook, you might come up with one of the floor plans on these two pages. These different treatments of the same space are also shown as elevation drawings.

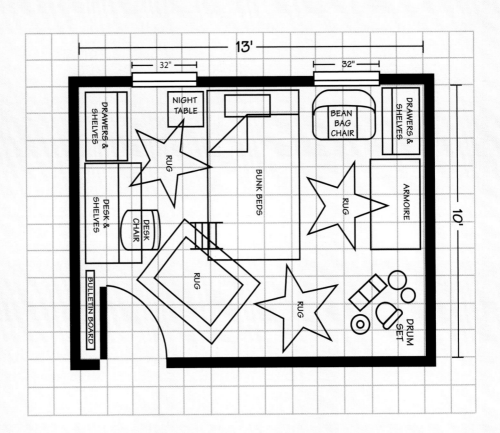

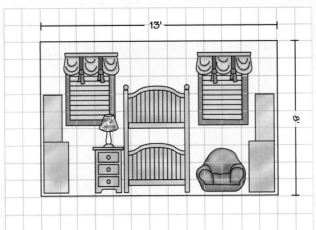

Plan A: intimate spaces

In this plan, the room functions as a retreat—for reading, daydreaming, doing schoolwork, and hanging out with a few good friends. The bunk bed divides the room into two separate spaces with a feeling of intimacy.

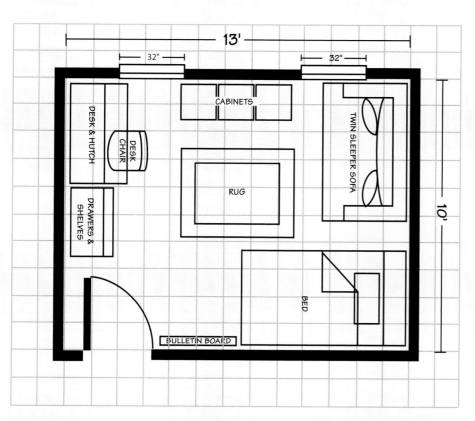

Plan B: a gathering place

This room design is modern and simple, with clean, uncluttered lines. It utilizes the whole space as a gathering place for many friends at once rather than dividing the room into separate activity areas.

Color *Palettes*

CREATING A COLOR SCHEME for your kid's room can be daunting. How can you be certain that the colors your child loves will work together in a room? Here are "real-life" color combinations that parents chose for the rooms shown in this book. The page number under each palette refers to the photo showcasing that palette. You can use these palettes as is, or you can alter them to fit your own room plan.

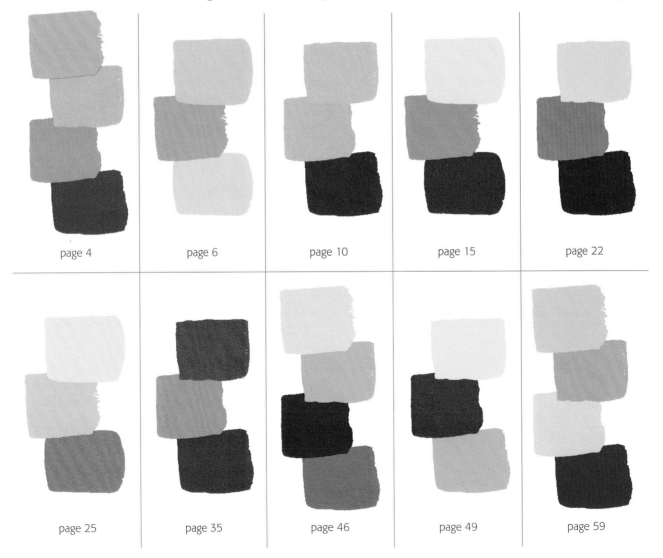

| page 4 | page 6 | page 10 | page 15 | page 22 |
| page 25 | page 35 | page 46 | page 49 | page 59 |

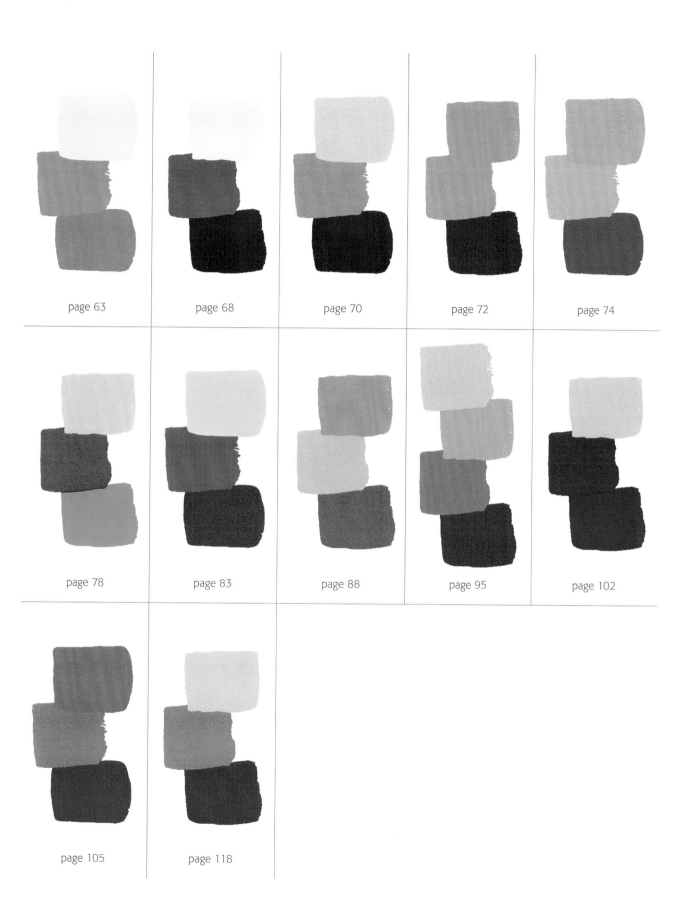

Design
and Photography Credits

DESIGN

Unless otherwise noted, the following credits are for interior design.

Front Matter

1 Patricia McDonald and Marcia Moore **2 left** Florence Goguely/Bille et Plume and Françoise Kirkman **2 right** Maison d'Etre **3 top** Sasha Emerson Design Studio **3 bottom** Swerve Co. of California and Goldin Design

Ideas and Inspiration

6 Maison d'Etre **7 left** Nancy Eslick **7 right** Karin Mason/Mason Designs **8** Lisa Malloy/Interior Inspirations **9 both** Architect: Alla Kazovsky **10–11 all** Kathy Claussen and Barbara Eddy/Superior Interiors **12 top and bottom left** Sasha Emerson Design Studio **12 right and 13 both** Decorative painting: Jeannie Lovell/Quinn-Art (www.quinn-art.com) **14–15 all** Furniture design: The Art of Furniture (www.danielhale.com) **16–17 all** Norm Claybaugh/Creative Interiors **18** Tent: IKEA **19** Magnetic strip: The Gardener; Shadow box display: Kathleen Navarra/Navarra Design Consultants; Chalkboard: Lighting Studio (www.lightingstudioberkeley.

com); Easel: The Land of Nod (www.landofnod.com) **20** Kerry Forbes **21 top** Lisa Malloy/Interior Inspirations **22** Philip J. Meyer, Ltd. and Shirley Robinson/Oliver's Collection (www.oliverscollection.com) **23 all** Swerve Co. of California and Goldin Design **24 top left and right** Decorative painting: Jeannie Lovell/Quinn-Art (www.quinn-art.com) **24 bottom** Furnishings: Ethan Allen **25** Claudia Fleury/Claudia's Designs **26** Loft bed: IKEA; Twin bed: Goodnight Room **27 bottom** Furnishings: IKEA **28 top** Kerry Forbes **28 bottom** Lisa Malloy/Interior Inspirations **29 top** Norm Claybaugh/Creative Interiors **31 left** Kathleen Navarra/Navarra Design Consultants **31 top right** Furnishings: Goodnight Room **31 bottom right** Furnishings: IKEA **32** Byron Kuth, Kuth/Ranieri Architects; Chris Whitney and Tommy Hicks/Objects Assembly **33 top** Swerve Co. of California and Goldin Design **33 bottom** Sasha Emerson Design Studio **35 left** Lisa Malloy/Interior Inspirations **35 top right** Ann Jones Interiors **35 bottom right** Sasha Emerson Design Studio **37 top** Gretchen Gibson and Jillann Wood/A Child's Eye View **37 bottom** Furniture design: The Art of Furniture (www.danielhale.com) **38 left** Gretchen Gibson and Jillann Wood/A Child's Eye View **38 right** Mark Dutka/InHouse Design Studio (www.inhousesf.com) **39** David Stark Wilson/Wilson Associates (www.dswdesign.com) **40** Occasional table:

Zinc Details (www.zincdetails.com); Nightstand and rolling table: IKEA; Play table and chairs: Goodnight Room; Child's set with chalkboard surface: Zinc Details (www.zincdetails.com) **41 all** Furnishings: IKEA **42** Rocker: Zinc Details (www.zincdetails.com); Foam cubes and pillows: IKEA **43** Beanbag chair: Ethan Allen; Easy chair and ottoman: The Land of Nod (www.landofnod.com); Modular chaise: Zinc Details (www.zincdetails.com); Swivel and straight-back chairs and rolling tractor seat: IKEA **44** Architecture: Michael Eserts and Grant Kirkpatrick/KAA Design Group (www.kaadesigngroup.com) **45 top** Florence Goguely/Bille et Plume and Françoise Kirkman **45 bottom** Mary Leigh Fitts **48 top and bottom left** Gretchen Gibson and Jillann Wood/A Child's Eye View **48 right and 49** Sasha Emerson Design Studio **50** Window treatment: Theresa Hernandez **51 left** Cindy Zelazny Rodenhaver **51 bottom right** Karin Mason/Mason Designs **52 top** Rug: IKEA **53 top** Patricia McDonald and Marcia Moore **53 bottom right** Barbara McQueen Interior Design **54** Braided and loop rugs: The Land of Nod (www.landofnod.com); Cut-pile rugs: IKEA **55 top right** Pammi Kapoor/Pamela Kapoor Interiors **55 bottom right** Rug design: Laura Armstrong **56** Trish Sheats/Thompson-Sheats Interior Design **57 top** RodMickley.com; Muralist: Bob Christian Decorative Art **57 bottom** Diane Chapman Interiors **59** Maison d'Etre **60 top right** Decorative painting: Jeannie Lovell/Quinn-Art (www.quinn-art.com) **60 left and bottom right** Norm Claybaugh/Creative Interiors **61** Heidi M. Emmett **62 top and bottom left** Philip J. Meyer, Ltd. and Shirley Robinson/Oliver's Collection

Index